PREFACE

May I put on record my appreciation of the helpful relations between Messrs. A. R. Mowbray as publishers and myself as author; of the expertise of the printers exhibited in the production of this book; of the permission granted me by the Oxford and Cambridge University Presses to make use of the New English Bible, Second Edition 1970; and last but not least of Mrs. J. Hodgson's skill and patience in producing a neat typescript from which the finished product has been made.

Kensington 1971 *D. W. Cleverley Ford*

CONTENTS

Introduction *page* 1

Sermon outlines for the seasons of the Church's year

ADVENT	Three kingdoms	3
	Understanding the Word	7
	Judgement	11
	Thanksgiving	13
CHRISTMAS	St. Matthew's Christmas sermon	16
	St. Luke's Christmas Exhibition	20
	Christ's star	22
EPIPHANY	A loophole	24
	Faith as a candle	27
	Christ the disclosure man	31
CONVERSION OF ST. PAUL	Our debt to St. Paul	35
SEPTUAGESIMA	Knowing the giver	38
SEXAGESIMA	Two gardens	42
QUINQUAGESIMA	The vision of the vertical	46
LENT	The mixture	49
	A hostile setting	52
	The test	55
	The mockers	58
	Passion pictures	62
PALM SUNDAY	The choice	66
GOOD FRIDAY	God is love	70

EASTER	Two halves	72
	The laughing angel	75
	Two ways of seeing	79
	Jesus or Christ	82
	The Christ of experience	85
	Bereavement is a storm	89
WHITSUNDAY	Catching the wind	91
WHITSUNTIDE	The Church of the future	94
TRINITY	Worship	96
AFTER TRINITY	Man's inner conflict	99
	The work of the Spirit	102
	Love	104
	Joy	106
	Peace	109
	Patience	111
	Kindness	113
	Goodness	116
	Fidelity	118
	Gentleness	120
	Self-control	122
ALL SAINTS' DAY	God's family	124

INTRODUCTION

As with my previous books on 'Preaching at the Parish Communion' this book has also been written at the invitation of the publishing department of Messrs. A. R. Mowbray of Oxford. The sales of those previous books appeared to indicate the usefulness of such tools for preachers—and they were no more than tools—with the result that I was asked to edit a forthcoming series of similar books by various writers and to launch it by contributing the first volume myself. Hence the present book entitled *Preaching through the Christian Year*.

What I have done this time is to break away from the Gospels and Epistles appointed for the Sundays and Saints' Days, indeed, away from any set scripture at all, but I have kept close to the teaching of the Church's year. I am sure such an adherence is wise and that for two reasons at least. First, it benefits the preacher. It gives him his subject and yet does not define it too closely. Creative work must have freedom to move. It also makes the preacher more comprehensive in the range of his preaching. The Christian year will not let him ride his own 'hobby-horse' very far. Secondly, it benefits the congregation. This applies particularly to a settled ministry in a settled place. It does mean that the congregation is given a balanced diet of Christian teaching.

I hope I have made this book interesting. Clearly, the production of outlines for sermons does not provide very great scope for lively and interesting presentation. But sermons have to be interesting as well as helpful. And so I have purposely betrayed myself here and there by *not* writing impersonally and I have not obliterated all references to my own environment.

It is not possible to preach well in a vacuum, it is doubtful if it is possible so to preach at all. Preaching is proclaiming the Kingdom of God to specific people in a specific place according to *their* need. We must, therefore, expect particularization in preaching and if we do not get it we are bored. Of course there are dangers. Preaching altogether is dangerous especially for the preacher. Yet the risks must be taken.

I remember an experience eighteen months ago when I was conducting a preaching school in Western Canada. Practice sermons were being preached to me in a low-roofed wooden church building by the side of the Trans-Canada Highway in a temperature of over 90°F. But it wasn't the heat which worried me so much as the preachers; and they, not because they wore the oddest assortment of clothes, indeed, very few clothes at all, to keep cool. What troubled me was that their sermons, otherwise carefully prepared and quite well delivered, nevertheless could as well have been preached in Brisbane, Bristol or the Barbados. They bore no obvious relation to British Columbia. No illustrations grounding the sermons in the life of the country were remotely discernible. I complained of course. It was my duty. And the next day, in the next bunch of preachers, I got my reward. A sermon using the overall image of the particular kind of tree on which the economy of the province largely depends, was both interesting and helpful. And having been shown some of those trees near the Lion Bridge in Vancouver through the kindness of those warm-hearted Canadian people, I have never forgotten it.

I hope this book will prove to be helpful. First of all to the clergy, many hundreds of whom it has been my privilege to meet in the last ten years and to talk with about preaching. And recently the circle has been widened to include ministers of Churches other than my own and of countries other than the United Kingdom. In addition to the clergy, the book may even have something to give to those who do not preach and do not need a tool for preaching. I dare to claim that what I have written here stems from experience, and who can define the limits of helpfulness when it is basic human experience that is being shared? Perhaps then this book will have something to say even outside the ranks of those whose burden and privilege it is to *preach* the Gospel. Such at least is my hope.

ADVENT

Three Kingdoms

Mark 1.15 (NEB) '*The time has come; the kingdom of God is upon you; repent, and believe the Gospel.*'

1. *Eschatology*

Today I am going to talk to you about eschatology. And you look at me as if I had taken leave of my senses. What on earth is eschatology? Is it animal, vegetable or mineral? And if we were playing Twenty Questions you would ask if a man could be a Christian without it. And I should have to reply 'yes'. And if you went on to press me: 'Could a man be an *informed* Christian without this thing?'—I should have to say 'no'. There is a sense in which a knowledge of eschatology is essential.

But what is it? What is eschatology? It is the doctrine of last things. 'Eschata' is Greek for 'last things' and 'logos' is Greek for 'teaching'.

And already your mind has shifted. You are wondering if those who take an interest in eschatology aren't 'cranky Christians' even 'crackpots'. In a way I am not surprised.

When I was in my early teens I was taken to see the ruins of a white stone tower. Scour my memory as I may, I can't think where, but I do recall how in the nineteenth century some people were so convinced of the nearness of the end of the world that they built this tower and assembled in it on the day they were convinced that the end would come. But it didn't. The special day dawned and passed like any other day. The milkman came round with the milk. The 9.30 pulled out of the station on time. That is why you label these people crackpots.

The difficulty, however, is that there is a fairly large amount of eschatology in the Bible. And in Advent we can't get away from it. 'What shall be the sign of thy coming and of the end of the world?' the disciples asked Jesus. And he went on to tell of nation rising against nation and kingdom against kingdom, of famines and earthquakes, of false Christs and false prophets. And as if this were not sufficient, eruptions in the natural order, the sun being darkened, the moon not giving her light, the stars falling from heaven. Yes, eschatology is in the Bible. There is a whole book on it, the book of the Revelation, sometimes called 'The Apocalypse'.

Now what are we to make of all this? Let me try to help you by telling you about three kingdoms, to all of which we might give the title 'Kingdom of God'.

2. *Three kingdoms*

First there was the kingdom of God established in Israel with the founding of the monarchy. No, you musn't laugh. Compared with the surrounding kingdoms of that time (a whole millennium before Christ), it really was like a fair lily rising up from the mud of a stagnant pool. J. M. Allegro may have written a lot of rubbish in his maddening book *The Sacred Mushroom and the Cross*, but he has at least made clear to all what some already knew that in some aspects the life of the Near Eastern world was like a cesspool of sexual preoccupation housed in religion. That a religion of pureness of living arose from such a milieu is one of the wonders of the world, but it did. In a very real sense the kingdom of old Israel was God's kingdom. In it God was honoured, his laws respected and transgressions punished. But it failed, of course. In spite of preachers (prophets) to keep it true to its principles it foundered. It split. It apostasized. It went into captivity. Granted it was never wholly lost, but neither did it ever wholly recover. And so in the darkest days of trial men's hope turned to the second kingdom of which I have to tell you.

This *second* kingdom is not in history at all. It is *beyond* history. It is at the end of history. It is not a kingdom of man's making but of God's making, 'a stone made without hands' as the book of Daniel calls it. So the idea took hold among the frustrations of the present of a kingdom of God beyond time, a kingdom of God at the end, a kingdom where God's power really would be manifest, his name honoured and his people would obediently walk in his ways without rebellion; a kingdom of peace and justice and universal brotherhood. This is the eschatological kingdom, the kingdom at the end, the kingdom for which the Victorians of whom I told you were waiting in the white stone tower they had built. And we mustn't rule out this idea of an eschatological kingdom, a kingdom of God at the end. If we do we are condemned to a view of history as for ever revolving in cycles, round and round with neither beginning nor end, and that takes all the purpose out of life. To use big words, to be meaningful life has to be teleological.

But there is a *third* way to think of God's kingdom. It is the way Jesus' whole life demonstrated. It is to see the future kingdom of God, the eschatological kingdom, as already come in Jesus. Listen to the first words of his preaching. 'The time has come; the kingdom of God is upon you; repent, and believe the Gospel.' Theologians call this eschatological preaching. And it was astonishing preaching, astonishing to those who first heard it. No wonder they assembled in droves to listen. Just think of it. They were looking for a kingdom at the end, beyond history, beyond time altogether, a kingdom where God's will would be done on earth as it is in heaven, where sins would be forgiven, God's peace granted, lost powers restored, new life begun, with death and deadness done away. And here was Jesus publicly asserting that that kingdom was already present. 'The time has come; the kingdom of God is upon you; repent, and believe the Gospel.'

And that I am bound to say is proper Christian preaching still. The powers of the age to come are available now through the Person of Christ.

In Jesus' day of course, men saw it with their own eyes. They saw the lame walk, the lepers cleansed, the deaf hear, even the dead raised up. The powers of the age to come were seen to be available in Galilee. God's kingdom was there, God's rule manifest, although the Romans occupied the country.

And after Christ's resurrection those same powers operated through the Apostles. Story after story in the book of the Acts of the Apostles recount this. And not even now has the whole tale been told, and never will be told till God's final kingdom comes, of how countless men and women have risen up through the power of Christ in their lives to trample down degrading self-centredness, joylessness and despair, even in the most adverse circumstances, and to kindle and display a light of life to all whom they encounter.

In Robert K. Massie's book *Nicolas and Alexandra* is a story of one of Russia's really great Christian women, the Grand Duchess Elizabeth, sister of the Empress Alexandra. Only God knows what she did for the poor and the underprivileged of her adopted country. But when revolution entered like fire into the hearts of the Russian peasants, as fire does, it did not stop at the general regard for this woman. The Provisional Government offered her refuge in the Kremlin, but she refused. Even the Kaiser tried several times through the Swedish Embassy, to bring the woman he once loved into the shelter of Germany. But she turned him down. Instead she went with other members of the Russian royal family to Alapayevsk in the Urals and was carried with them in a peasant cart to the mouth of an abandoned mine shaft. Still alive, they were thrown down the shaft. Heavy timbers and hand grenades were thrown on top to complete the work. Not all the victims were killed immediately, for a peasant who crept up to the pit after the murderers had left heard hymns being sung at the bottom of the shaft. Later, when the bodies were removed, the injured head of one of the boys was found carefully bound with a handkerchief. It belonged to the Grand Duchess Elizabeth, affectionately known as 'Ella'.

3. *The Advent Message*

Here then is the Advent message, the powers of the age to come, the power to overcome hate, bitterness, resentment, weakness and sin, even to bring and provide succour in face of terrible anguish and adversity, is present now through faith in the crucified and risen Christ. Our salvation lies in repentance and faith, because the time has come, the kingdom of God is at hand, or in the words of St. Paul. 'The night is far spent, the day is at hand; let us therefore cast off the works of darkness, let us put upon us the armour of light.'

ADVENT

Understanding the Word

> Acts 8.31 (NEB) '"*Do you understand what you are reading?*" *He said,* "*How can I understand unless someone will give me the clue?*"'

INTRODUCTION

On October 3rd 1932 I was sitting in a railway train bound for Liverpool Street station. I was about to set out on the life of a theological student, not knowing at all where it would lead me. But I wanted to achieve as high an academic standard as I could, so I thought I would use the three-hour journey to read the Greek Testament, having just mastered the first steps in that language. Half-way to London the carriage filled up and a man sat down beside me. Presently he began to look over my shoulder at my little book, obviously puzzled, obviously intrigued. Finally, he could withhold himself no longer and said, 'Do you understand what you are reading?' And I, greatly daring, said, 'Yes, I think so, at least I am getting on.' Then he told me he was a clergyman in mufti, asked me where I was going, and gave me an introduction. Not so very long ago I met that same clergyman again, having never encountered him since 1932. I introduced myself and told him my story. 'Do you remember' I said, 'the boy in the train reading the Greek Testament, and you asked if he could understand what he was reading?' But not a flicker of recognition crossed his eyes. Apparently he had forgotten everything about it. I don't blame him. . . .

Today I bring to your notice a man riding in a carriage and reading the scriptures. He was a well set-up man, a coloured man, probably returning from some diplomatic mission to Jerusalem. He had a long journey in front of him all the way down the coast road to the Gaza Strip, on to Egypt and on further south still into Africa, mile after mile, league after league. And to while away the time on his bumpy journey, he was reading the book of the prophet Isaiah. Perhaps his brow was furrowed. Perhaps every now and again he heaved a sigh as he struggled with Isaiah's literary phrases written in the Hebrew tongue. And then we can imagine a face appearing at the carriage window, a pleasant face, an eager face, clearly not out for money. 'Do you understand what you are reading?' he asked. And the answer from the traveller came back straight and honest. 'How can I understand unless someone will give me the clue?'

1. *We need the clue*

And that is always true of the Bible. We cannot understand it unless we are given the clue. The Bible is a long book and a difficult book. The span of time in which it was written lasted over a thousand years and many hands took a part in writing it and editing it. It contains history, poetry, moral precepts and letters, yes and other types of writing too, with complicated names like 'apocalyptic'. How shall we understand it? We never shall—unless we are given the clue. And the clue is Christ, God in Christ. That is what the whole Bible is about. The old Testament climbs up a long hill to this summit at its end: the birth, life, death and resurrection of Christ. Then it flows out and onward again through the New Testament. That is to say, the summit is in the middle, it is even concentrated in the story of one solitary weekend, the Friday when Christ was crucified, and the Sunday following, when the same Christ was raised from the grave. That event is the clue to the Bible. Everything in the way of understanding turns on that *one* point, seeing that its purpose is to make God real to us.

But we have to be shown this. The aristocratic coloured man riding in his chariot down by the Gaza Strip had to be shown it. And since the friendly face at the carriage window seemed to be so eager he invited him to join him in the chariot to explain. And that is another picture I would love to paint if I were an artist. Philip the evangelist, God's man in mufti sitting beside the high official of the Ethiopian Queen explaining the words Isaiah wrote. 'He was led as a lamb to the slaughter, and as a sheep before her shearers is dumb, so he opened not his mouth.' And then the question 'Of whom speaketh the prophet this?' It was the evangelist's chance which he took at once, telling him the good news of Jesus. It was the clue that the reader needed.

2. *We need an interpreter*

We all need the Bible in our Christian faith. It won't remain *Christian* faith for very long unless it is constantly informed by what the Bible has to say. But the Bible itself needs an interpreter. Every one of us needs someone to mount up into his chariot of life as it bowls bumpily along, for we shall not understand it unless we are given the clue. This is why we need *biblically based* preaching. How we need it today! This is the value to be gained from the *Bible Reading Fellowship;* and one of the most extraordinary things that has happened in England during the last twelve months is that some hundreds of Roman Catholics have joined and are reading the notes, an almost unheard of thing in history. Roman Catholic lay people studying the Bible. And we also need *study groups* where they can be held. Every Christian needs a guide in reading the Bible. 'How can I understand unless someone will give me the clue?'

3. *The issue is action*

But my story doesn't end with a two-man study group in a carriage bumping down the Gaza Strip. It culminates in action as all true study ought to do. The official suddenly lifted his eyes from the Hebrew characters of Isaiah's scroll, and from the honest face of his unexpected tutor. Out through the window he spied water, which you do not often see in a desert. 'Look', he said, 'Water! Couldn't I be baptized?' And my guess is that the coachman up on 'the box' kept on rubbing his eyes and pinching his arms, making sure he wasn't dreaming. His master, the Queen's official, walking out to be baptized down there by the roadside, where anyone might stop and stare.

This is the point. The reading, the studying, the talking, led not simply to a theory, but to a person, a personal God, a God calling him to action. And he took it. He sealed himself in with God's people, something more than simply changing his mind. And so his Bible reading was effective, effective in his life. He answered the call of the God he met.

4. *Further possibilities*

Finally, these travellers bid each other their farewell. Did they ever meet again? Did the official ever make another diplomatic journey to Jerusalem, and did he run across this man called Philip, Philip the Evangelist? It seems unlikely, but if he did do you think that no flicker of recognition would pass across the evangelist's face? Of course he remembered. And my guess is that the coloured official remembered too, remembered every detail. And here is a thought that has never ceased to intrigue my mind. Ethiopia in Africa, from which this official came, and where he was returning as a baptized man, has been a Christian State, unlike her neighbouring states in Africa, for many hundreds of years. Could it be that this official, fresh from his Bible reading in the chariot, began the Church's mission in his homeland? If so, what an amazing sequel! But you never know what will be the outcome when people learn to read the Bible with the clue. It can lead to striking results and very often does.

ADVENT

Judgement

A boy stood in the juvenile court room being questioned. Whether or not he was disconcerted was hard to tell. There was in fact no light in his eye, and if there ever had been it had long since gone out. Perhaps his answers to the questions supplied the reason.

'Did your father know you were out till the early hours of the morning?'

'No.'

'Did either of your parents have any idea of the kind of company you had been keeping?'

'I don't know.'

'What do you think they would have done if they had known you had frequently been engaged in shoplifting?'

'I don't think they would have cared one way or the other.'

1. *The good news of God's judgement*

Almost the worst conclusion that a boy could come to about his parents is that they do not care whether he chooses wrong or right. A parent who (a) has no opinion of right or wrong, (b) does not take any action upon his opinion with reference to his children, is callous in the extreme, unworthy of the name parent. Similarly, if God is not a God of judgement he is no God worthy of human respect. To hear then that God is a God of judgement is good news. There is even a Gospel of God's wrath. This is the Advent message.

2. *God acts upon his judgement now*

In other words, judgement is a present process. How does God judge? Not by hurling thunder-bolts out of the blue. God gives us what we ask. That is how he judges. One of the strongest expressions of this occurs in Psalm 106 verse 15, where having told of the Israelites tempting God in the desert, the comment is made, 'He gave them their desire:

and sent leanness withal into their soul.' There can be no doubt that God is judging the western world at present. By and large, it seeks little beyond material wealth and God does not hinder it from obtaining that upon which it has set its heart. The West prospers, but its soul has become a wretched, shrinking, half-starved thing. 'God gave them their desire: and sent leanness withal into their soul.' That is the judgement.

3. *There is a day of future judgement*

To assert this does not altogether fit in with the predilections of the modern mind. We like to think in terms of evolution, like to think of processes, are half-afraid of any suggestion of finality. But we cannot assert that the Bible does not look towards a final day of judgement. There is to be an end of history. There is to be an ultimate dénouement of all that is evil and an ultimate vindication of all that is good.

* * *

God is a God of judgement, that is to say, he differentiates between good and evil, cleanness and dirt, day and night, life and death. There are absolutes. Not everything is relative. And not only does God act in judgement some time, he acts in judgement now, in history, in life, in the world we know and see and touch and smell. God is active in judgement here. But not only here, but one day finally as well. It will be a ratification of what has been going on all the time.

'The Lord is a God of judgement' (Isaiah 30.18). Is this a hard saying? It is certainly a strong saying. But is it a hard saying? On the contrary, it is very comforting, for if God did not judge, how could we possibly say he cared? And care he certainly does for 'God sent not his son into the world to condemn the world, but that the world through him might be saved.' (John 3.17).

ADVENT

Thanksgiving

Philippians 4.6 '*In everything, by prayer and supplication with thanksgiving, let your requests be made known unto God.*'

INTRODUCTION

At the far end of Launceston Place a new three-storied town house is being erected. There is nothing very remarkable about that; nor about the large pile of sand pitched from a lorry into the roadway nearby; nor about the bags of cement, nor about this fact, because it is a fact, that those bricks which will comprise the house couldn't be laid with the sand alone, nor with the cement alone, nor even by mixing the sand and cement together and applying it alone. The whole operation is conditioned by the availability and use of water. It is water that makes sand and cement bind for use in bricklaying.

1. *The binding element*

Now in the words of St Paul given to the Christians in Philippi about prayer there lies a similar basic necessity. In all the prayers, supplications and requests that make up the devotions, thanksgiving must be the all-pervasive binding activity. 'In everything, by prayer and supplication *with thanksgiving*, let your requests be made known unto God, and the peace of God. . . . shall guard your hearts and your thoughts in Christ Jesus.' Prayers without thanksgiving will not lead to the peace of God. Thanksgiving is the essential cohesive force in all our praying.

Some time ago I heard Quintin Hogg, as he then was, give the 'Ten to Eight' religious talk on radio. I am not always impressed by these talks, but I was held by this one. It was about the Te Deum. Apparently Quintin Hogg loves the Te Deum. It does not matter if it is said in a village church, chanted in a town church, or sung to a glorious setting in a cathedral, he loves the Te Deum. 'We praise thee, O God: we acknowledge thee to be the Lord. All the earth doth worship thee: the Father everlasting.' And this was the reason he gave. It is the characteristic hymn of the Church. Other movements have their characteristic hymns. 'Land of Hope and Glory' for one political party, the 'Red Flag Song' for another, the 'Marseillaise' for revolutionary France, 'John Brown's Body' for the United States; but for the Christian Church the characteristic hymn is, or should be, the Te Deum. And we in our Church here ought especially to be aware of this because the words of the Te Deum are written all around the interior of this building at the point where the tops of the walls touch the red ceiling, beginning appropriately over the choir:

Te Deum laudamus
Te Dominum confitemur

Symbolically, thanksgiving is a ring round our building, binding all our worship together.

2. *The heart of worship*

Let me make one other point on this. In the Communion service we proceed through the service quietly and reflectively till we come to what is called the 'Sursum Corda' and this should be different. I always say it boldly and loudly and I expect a bold and loud congregational reply as a result.

'Lift up your hearts.'
'We lift them up unto the Lord.'
'Let us give thanks unto our Lord God.'
'It is meet and right so to do.'

And then you will notice how the liturgy proceeds. 'It is very meet, right, and our bounden duty, that we should at all times, and in all places, give thanks unto thee, O Lord, Holy Father, Almighty, Everlasting God.'

That is to say, anyone who professes to be a Christian should be regular and constant in his thanksgiving. The very word 'Eucharist' means thanksgiving. It is the heart of our worship. 'In everything, by prayer and supplication with thanksgiving, let your requests be made known unto God.'

3. *The root is acceptance*

And some-one is thinking 'Yes that is all right when everything is going well.' I was talking to a man on Friday who seemed unusually cheerful and I discovered it was because his daughter had recently got married and all seemed to be working out very well. But what is required of the Christian is *daily* thanksgiving, in other words, a constant attitude.

I think I really understood what this means from a paperback I picked up in W. H. Smith's bookshop a few days ago called *Markings* by Dag Hammarskjöld, the former Secretary General of the United Nations. Hammarskjöld was a sincere Christian who kept a spiritual diary, and this is what *Markings* is. In this book he frequently points out that the way to face life, the way to face each day of life, each circumstance of life is with a 'yes'. We say 'yes' to the day of cloudless sunshine, that is easy, though not everyone does it. But we should also say 'yes' to the day of rain and storm, 'yes' to the day of bristling problems, and here surely Hammarskjöld must have known what he was talking about. For weeks on end he had to work a twenty-hour day—yes, and through illness and disappointment, nevertheless as the Psalm puts it, 'This is the day which the Lord hath made, let us rejoice and be glad in it.' To begin each day in that attitude of acceptance constitutes the whole binding force of prayer. Prayer begins and is crowned not by petition, 'O God give me', but by an attitude. 'It is very meet, right, and our bounden duty, that we should at all times, and in all places, give thanks unto thee, O Lord, Holy Father, Almighty, Everlasting God.'

This does not mean quiescence, it does not mean sitting down under all difficulties, injustices and obstacles. Perhaps the meaning can best be described in what is sometimes called the 'serenity prayer'—'O Lord, give me grace to change what needs to be changed, to accept what cannot be altered, and the wisdom to know the difference.'

There are two words representing two attitudes which need to be set clearly over against each other. The one is resentment and the other is thanksgiving. This is the point. We may not like the difficult thing. We may not understand why it has come; we may long to be free of it. It may hurt terribly, it may cause us sleepless nights. The wrong thing, however, is to resent it. The right thing is to say 'yes' to it. This is how life is, the life that God has made.

A few days ago I read this Indian proverb: 'I heard a man grumbling because he had no shoes, then he saw a man with no feet.' To which we might add. 'I grumbled because the sky was so dark, and then I saw a blind child who would never see the sky at all. . . .'

'In everything, by prayer and supplication with thanksgiving. . . .'

'Lift up your hearts.'
'It is meet and right so to do.'

CHRISTMAS

St Matthew's Christmas Sermon

INTRODUCTION

One evening late in October as the autumn mists were gathering in the London streets, two middle-aged men sat opposite each other in a club in St James's, one slightly older than the other. They were deep in conversation, if you could call that a conversation in which one was doing most of the talking. The elder was describing vividly an enterprise in a Midland town in which he was obviously interested; its origin, its development and its current resources. But the younger was puzzled. The story was captivating enough in its way, but why was it being recounted to *him*? It could not be simply for the sake of the story. And so he asked, almost bluntly, and received this answer, 'Because I am hoping to persuade you to accept a job with this firm.'

The story which we hear recounted every Christmas is originally told in two places, and only two. Two chapters of St Matthew's Gospel and two chapters of St Luke's Gospel. But why do they tell it? Is it simply for the sake of the story? Or is it because the writers wish to persuade us to take up a certain attitude to the central figure, the Christ Child? And the answer, of course, is 'yes'. What in fact these two writers are doing is proclaiming the good news of Jesus Christ by means of the story of his birth. In a way, what they are each doing is preaching a sermon, a Christian sermon.

Now like hundreds of other clergymen, I have prepared many sermons, in my case at least three thousand. And I, like them, know this about sermons. There has to be solid content. There has to be a carefully prepared shape or form. There also has to be a clear-cut aim. And the same three ingredients will be found in St Matthew's and St Luke's stories of the birth of Jesus. There is a solid historical basis. There is a carefully worked out literary presentation. There is also the underlying aim to influence readers to adopt an attitude of faith in Jesus. I can't tell you where exactly the solid historical basis begins and ends in these stories, who can? But that *the writers* believed the Virgin Birth actually took place cannot be gainsaid.

THE INTENTION OF ST MATTHEW

What then did St Matthew intend us to think about Jesus as a result of his story of the birth?

1. *A new beginning*

First that with the coming of this child a new beginning was made for the human race. This point can be checked. The opening words of the Gospel actually read in the Greek 'The book of the *genesis* of Jesus Christ'. And in verse eighteen of Chapter 1, 'Now the *genesis* of Jesus Christ was like this.' The word 'genesis' means 'beginning'. Who can doubt then that the first book in the *New* Testament looks back to the first book of the *Old* Testament, which is the book of Genesis. And as Genesis tells of the old creation, so St Matthew tells of the new creation. As Genesis tells of how the Spirit of God brooded upon the waters, so St Matthew tells of how the Spirit of God overshadowed Mary. Thus at the first Christmas there took place a new start for men and women everywhere. Or as Newman's hymn expresses it:

> 'A second Adam to the fight
> And to the rescue came.'

2. *A new focus*

A second aim of St Matthew's Christmas sermon is to show Jesus as the Son of David. Once again we look at the opening words of the book. 'The book of the genesis of Jesus Christ the *Son of David*.' And before we reject this as a piece of irrelevant antiquarianism, we must realise what a ring it had in every Hebrew ear. 'Son of David' summed up men's noblest ideals. It was the answer to men's deepest longings, in fact 'all the hope of all the years' were looked for in some descendant of this fascinating King of Israel; and, said St Matthew, he was born to Mary. No wonder men's hearts stirred at the news when it was proclaimed in *these terms*. Here was no upstart, no creature of the moment, no product of some revolutionary coup, but a true son descended of the royal house through Joseph. Granted as far as Joseph was concerned, Jesus was his adopted child (said Matthew), but God had worked before for Israel by strange exceptional happenings. Think of Tamar, Rahab, Ruth and Bathsheba. Make no mistake, this is God's child answering to men's brightest ideals, the focus of their deepest hopes.

3. *A new worker*

A third aim of St Matthew's Christmas sermon is to present Jesus not simply as the focus for human aspirations, but as a strenuous worker himself, active on behalf of men. To do this, St Matthew structured his story on the story of Moses in the book of Exodus. Herod sought Jesus' life as a child, and Pharaoh sought the life of Moses as a child. Jesus was rescued by his parents fleeing to Egypt, and Moses had been saved by his mother by the waters of the Egyptian river and finally fled from Egypt. Moses led his people through the Red Sea in order to open up a new home in Canaan. Jesus, too, overcame 'the sharpness of death, and opened the kingdom of heaven to all believers.' Who can doubt that St Matthew is preaching a sermon on Jesus' birth, using the story of Moses as a text? What for? To show that what happened at Jesus' cradle was the birth of a greater one than Moses, fashioning an even greater deliverance.

4. *Appeal*

Here, then, is St Matthew's invitation at Christmas time—to look into the story of Jesus' birth and see something absolutely new: a new beginning for the human race, a new focus for men's highest ideals, a new worker on man's behalf over against his direst foes of sin and death.

Can we not trust this new Saviour? Can we not commit our souls to him? And the answer prises itself out of our modern lips, 'Not yet'. And no wonder. The cradle scene is too tender for strong reliance, too savouring of the sentimental to bear the weight of long frustrated hopes and fears. But St Matthew has not finished all he has to say. The tale is not told on Christmas Day alone. Soon we shall be standing outside a city wall, gazing up at what men did to Jesus with a gibbet, but how he rose again, triumphant. Then maybe with humbled minds, creep back we shall to this small cradle scene, this manger scene, the straw upon the ground, those cattle breathing heavily as cattle do, to see the baby, in a different way, the Christ with different eyes. Then maybe we shall kneel down low to worship, then to laugh and sing his praises. This babe is Christ the Lord, the Saviour of the human race—yes, and our Saviour too, if we let him, the Saviour of the nineteen-seventies.

CHRISTMAS

St Luke's Christmas Exhibition

1. *Everyman's exhibition*

At this time of year almost every home arranges an improvised picture exhibition. It may be on the mantelpiece. It may spread over the bookshelves and on to the top of the piano. Some people string it out on a line across the room or dangle it on coloured ribbon from the picture rail (I don't like this idea). But however it is displayed there is no variability about the contents. It consists of Christmas cards; and for the most part Christmas cards are pictures, some of them attractive, others not so attractive.

2. *St Luke's exhibition*

Now at Christmas time St Luke set out for us in his Gospel an exhibition of *seven pictures*. They are in two groups, four on one side and three on the other; the odd arrangement being intentional because picture number three is connected with both sides. In a way there are two Christmas triptychs and one extra picture. Let us walk round the exhibition. First, the annunciation to Zechariah of the birth of a son to Elizabeth, then the annunciation to Mary of the birth of a son to herself; next, the meeting of the two mothers (the picture that belongs to both groups); then the miraculous birth of John. And now, the second collection of pictures. First, the miraculous birth of Jesus, then the presentation of Jesus in the Temple, and finally the visit to the Temple of Jesus at the age of twelve, the last occasion when 'the Holy Family' were together as far as our records are concerned.

3. *The point of the exhibition*

Why did St Luke arrange these pictures? Is it that they simply happened to come into his possession just as Christmas cards come into ours, and we set them up on the mantelpiece, or did he arrange them in some special order so that he might say something about Jesus? There can be no doubt that the latter is the truth. Purpose is obvious from the arrangement. Two miraculous births, one to a woman past child-bearing age, the other to a woman who was a virgin. Two mothers meeting. Two songs of praise concerning each child, the Benedictus for John, the Magnificat for Jesus. And two receptions of the children. John among his family at his circumcision, Jesus in the Temple with no wide family circle at all, and an offering of only two pigeons, the poor man's gift.

4. *The message of the exhibition*

And what was St Luke saying about Jesus by this exhibition? That the importance of the child lies in his destiny to be the great shepherd of all men, something calling for loudest praise. Perhaps of all the pictures, the fifth in the exhibition holds the clue. It is in Chapter two verse eleven. 'Today in the city of David a deliverer has been born to you—the Messiah, the Lord.' He was not a strange saviour, not an upstart deliverer with no background. This one belongs to the city of David. His roots stretch down in an impeccable pedigree. His own immediate tale starts in a priestly family obeying a ritual order (Zechariah). This deliverer does not seize his position, he inherits it. But it is not empty authority. It is personal as well. He can stand up to doctors of the law at the age of twelve in the Temple itself. And what is more significant than everything, his mission is not for Jewry alone, he is to be 'a light to lighten the Gentiles' as well as the glory of God's people Israel. So this Jesus was born in Bethlehem, the city of David, the great Shepherd King, and the first to visit him were shepherds from David's fields— Why? Because this child born in a manger is the great shepherd of his people everywhere. The angel choir sang his praises 'Glory to God in the highest'. Yes, the Church's liturgical hymn is appropriate even for celestial lips. It tells of one greater than all in the scope of his service, God's deliverer for everyman.

5. *The application of the message*

Is not this the great lesson to grasp at Christmas? Too often we restrict Jesus. Too often we think of him only as a Saviour of the Church. But he is the world's Saviour. The Saviour of society, the Saviour of civilization. People cannot live together in peace and security unless they take the Christ spirit into their life, otherwise grab and grasp, exploitation and expropriation, death and destruction become the order of the day, no matter how sophisticated we grow. Christ is the Saviour destined for all men. That is the message of St Luke's exhibition of seven pictures. Will we hear that message today? Will we sing this Deliverer's praises? Will we make him our Saviour?

CHRISTMAS

Christ's star

Christmas must have its star. A star belongs to Christmas, and Christmas belongs to a star. But that is not quite correct. What St Matthew describes is *Christ's star*. Note the text carefully (Matthew 2.2, NEB), '. . . astrologers from the east arrived in Jerusalem, asking, "Where is the child who is born to be king of the Jews? We observed the rising of *his star*. . . ." '

Did Christ have a star? I mean, did a star appear at his birth? I do not see why not. But whether it was Halley's comet which appeared in 11 BC, or the rare conjunction of Saturn and Jupiter, said by Kepler to have appeared in 7 BC, I do not know. But the star, whatever it was, certainly did not go 'ahead of the wise men until it stopped above the place where the child lay'. Such is not possible for a star millions of light years distant. It cannot pinpoint a cradle. What St Matthew has given us is a *symbolic* use of an *historical* event, what the Jews called Midrash. And when we understand this we are able to receive the lessons of this scripture. What are they?

First, that Christ's birth can infuriate

This is brought out by the emphasis on Herod in the story. You can't get away from Herod. His name occurs nine times in Chapter 2 of St Matthew's Gospel. And it is Herod as an enemy. The star turned him into an enemy. Strictly speaking it was the astrologers' interpretation of the star that had that effect. They said the star was concerned with the birth of a king. And Herod took them seriously. All the ancient world took the horoscope seriously. It was common belief to reckon each new-born babe had his star. There were thousands of thousands of babies. But there are thousands of thousands of stars. And your star determined your fortune. Some people still believe this. They think they have a lucky star or unlucky star. The astrologers in this story saw Christ's star as indicating kingship. And it maddened Herod. It turned him into an enemy. He was not going to have this child reign over him, just as some people today will not have this Christ as controller of their morals or their money, or any of their ways. . . .

Secondly, Christ's birth can call to worship
It called the wise men to the opposite of fury. Verse eleven is striking in this story about the astrologers. 'At the sight of the star they were overjoyed.' Joy is the proper Christian reaction. Joy over the birth of a ruler who will care for people. And the joy led on to worship, and worship to the offering of rich symbolic gifts. So we see Christ's birth as divisive. Some people like Herod, turn to hate. Some, like the wise men, turn to joyfulness. Who can doubt what is the right reaction?

Thirdly, Christ's birth led to Christ's victory
And this is strange because the path to his victory was not straight. It went round by the Cross. Herod plotted and Herod struck, but he did not kill the infant Christ. The Jews struck, the Romans struck. They hanged up Jesus on a cross, but though he died he was not beaten, he rose victorious from the grave. So from afar men came to see him as their Lord. This is the overwhelming lesson of the story St Matthew gives in the second chapter of his Gospel. Christ's star never sets. It goes on shining brightly, come what may. That is why we should always place a star on the top of every Christmas tree. It stands for Christ. He overtops the world. It is our symbol of rejoicing.

APPLICATION

So here we see two sets of people with two reactions: Herod and his soldiers with their swords and the wise men with their gifts. And in between the star. Which side is yours? Which group holds your allegiance? Let Christmas be a time for fresh alignment to the wise men's attitude. It is the inner secret of our joy at Christmas time.

EPIPHANY

A loophole

INTRODUCTION

The story you have just heard—the turning by Jesus of the water into wine—is one of which many commentators make heavy weather. The stumbling block is the triviality of the occasion. How different, or so it seems to these commentators, if the powers of Jesus had been exercised to feed a hungry crowd of men and women; how satisfying if he had given of himself to drive back the ravages of some devastating disease; but what we have instead is the alleged production of gallons and gallons of wine for guests at a village wedding who had already drunk more than enough. What sort of a miracle is this? What sort of Christ does this portray?

1. *A miracle in the commonplace*

I see their point, but sometimes I wonder. I can't imagine some mother in Kensington counting it a matter of no consequence if at the wedding of her daughter the champagne gave out. I can't imagine *anyone* in this part of London thinking it does not really matter if a party turned out to be a flop. Maybe we have got our perspectives wrong. Maybe, after all, simple domestic concerns are as important to God as committee meetings at the United Nations. Maybe what things constitute a woman's anxieties are of equal concern to our

Lord as the massive problems of State confronting Mr Nixon. Maybe we ought to take comfort, and especially the women here in this congregation, when St John informs us that Christ wrought his first miracle at Cana of Galilee at a wedding reception solving a domestic problem.

2. *The problem in denying miracles*

But look a little closer. Was it a miracle? If so, can we accept the Gospel miracles? You see, I am now talking like a twentieth-century man. I am not asking '*Did* Jesus turn the water into wine?' I am asking '*Could* Jesus have turned the water into wine?' In other words, can miracles happen?

For a long time now, a hundred years, perhaps, there has developed a strong opinion that every effect has a cause, and every cause has an effect, in the sense that both cause and effect are locked together in a closed circuit relationship. And if in the past ten years or so there has come to be recognized in physics what is called a principle of *indeterminacy*, the great mass of people, more especially men, influenced by science, reckon miracles ruled out. The universe works with fixed laws, like a machine. There is no possibility of an exception. So Jesus did not turn the water into wine. The action is impossible, except by absorbing water through the stem, branches and fruit of the vine.

What do we say to this? We can say, it is logical to say, that if miracles are impossible, impossible even for God, then God is restricted by his own creation. In other words, God is a prisoner, God has no freedom, the laws of natural cause and effect have the last word, even for him. Freedom then does not exist. It is impossible, and the matter is in no way eased by trying to assert that God does not exist either.

So you see what we are up against if we say that miracles are impossible. We are up against the idea that *freedom* is impossible and what we imagine is human freedom does not really exist at all. So what becomes of the modern cry for freedom now being voiced from every quarter. Freedom for the workers, freedom for the students, freedom for the coloured races, freedom for the under-privileged. Go and tell these people that freedom is nothing but wishful thinking, what will they say?

And someone wants to raise his voice: 'This is all too clever, all too philosophical for a Sunday morning in church.' All right. I will therefore concentrate the point by saying 'Be very careful how you say miracles cannot happen or you may find yourself occupying an untenable position.'

3. *What a miracle is*

What then is a miracle? How can we describe one of these miracles from the Gospels such as the one brought to our attention on this second Sunday after the Epiphany? A miracle is a loophole, a tiny slit in the stout fortress walls of human existence through which we can catch a tiny glimpse of an altogether different level and potentiality of existence.

How does the story of the water turned into wine in the Gospel end? It ends with these words, 'This first miracle Jesus wrought in Cana of Galilee and manifested forth his glory. And his disciples believed in him.' In other words, that miracle was an epiphany, it was a disclosure point of existence of a transcendent life so different from the natural order that we can only call it supernatural, what is called the glory of Christ.

APPLICATION

I think we must believe this. I am not saying that I think it will matter very much whether you believe that the miracle story we heard this morning took place literally as it was described. But I think it will matter a very great deal whether or not you believe that the natural order is all there is and no spiritual power exists or is effective from beyond it. Because if that is so, it is little use praying, little use worshipping, little use coming to the sacrament of God's real presence at the Holy Communion table. At best they can only be described as useful psychological exercises. But if we believe that God is, that God is an active God, that God does things, even hears us thinking, how different the most ordinary day looks.

Is not this the significance of the story of the wedding ceremony at Cana? Mary voiced her prayer about a very ordinary lack, 'They have no wine.' And Christ heard it. And Christ answered. What a lesson! In the midst of ordinary everyday life there is a divine potentiality available, even to a woman's prayer, able to transform situations. That is the power we seek in our Church today. It is the dynamic of the supernatural available in Christ.

EPIPHANY

Faith as a candle

> Psalm 18.28 '*Thou also shalt light my candle: the Lord my God shall make my darkness to be light.*'

In many of our churches at Epiphany we light extra candles. Not because the January daylight is meagre though that may be so; not because we count our church interiors particularly in need of brightening up, though this could be the case; but in order to provide a symbolic presentation of a truth which Epiphany brings to our attention, that God is light.

1. *The small light of faith*

But how is God a light to us? What kind of a light? There can be little doubt, I think, that our theoretical answer would be that God is a great light, he is 'the light of the world'. But that is not how we experience him. We experience God normally as a small light, almost as a candle. 'Thou also shalt light my candle: the Lord my God shall make my darkness to be light.'

During the electricians' go-slow, many thousands of people all over the country had the experience, for some part of the enforced darkness at least, of living by the light of a candle. What a small light a candle provides! It does not illuminate a whole room. It does not illuminate even a whole desk-top, as I discovered. But you can get along with a candle. You can write letters with a candle. You can find your way in a room by its very small light.

Our experience of God is normally like that. We know him as a small light. Which means, of course, that because we are believers in God, we shall not, therefore, know all the answers about life. To none of us will be imparted the reasons why some suffer and others do not; why certain men lost their lives at a Glasgow football ground and many thousands of others arrived home quite safe and sound. None of us knows what kind of a world it will be in which our grandchildren must make their way. And not even the most saintly can tell us what lies on the other side of the frontier-post called death. We live, so to speak, even as believing men and women, by the light of a candle, no more, no less.

And you must know that with a candlelight, there are always mysterious shadows on the walls, always pools of darkness beyond the arm's length. In fact, even with the candle in our hands, we still walk largely by faith and not by sight. So it is with our experience of God as a general rule. But this also we know, how dark it was for those in December who had no candle at all, how incapacitating. Faith in God provides maybe only a small light, but without that faith, how very dark it is.

2. *Alternative lights*

At this point, of course, any logical mind would have to remind us that in our modern world we have greatly improved on candles, indeed, they only survive for ceremonial purposes. May it not be so with faith in God? Could it also be described as a picturesque relic of a bygone age? Could we be said to have advanced beyond it?

This is the argument of the humanist and especially of the scientific humanist today. There have been other times when this line of thought appealed. One such period was the eighteenth century. It was even called the Age of Enlightenment and Voltaire was its apostle, the apostle of reason. But this alternative to the light of faith, this light of reason, failed. It was superseded in the dark, rebellious moods of men that followed when instinct, feeling, passion and impulse were thought to be the proper lights of life. So the great Romantic Movement got under way. But this, too, ran out into the twilight of disillusionment.

In our day we have seen quite a few lights flicker and fail. What glorious hopes, for example, the natural sciences engendered, and not surprisingly. After all, what benefits technology has brought, but what problems too! And natural philosophy and metaphysics, once the background thinking of every educated man, have all but disappeared. And an ordered, planned, social existence with recognizable and accepted patterns of behaviour, easing the social intercourse of people in general has all but been obliterated by a thrusting, grasping, anarchical approach, sometimes irrationally stimulated by drugs. On all which attempts to produce sparks of light supposedly more up-to-date and effective than the small light of faith in God, a verse from Isaiah seems aptly to comment. 'Walk in the light of your fire, and among the sparks that ye have kindled. This shall ye have at my hand, ye shall lie down in sorrow.' (Isaiah 50.11).

3. *The light of life*

But the Bible does not spell out sadness, but rather is shot through with a triumphant note; and this is the message of Epiphany. 'And the Gentiles shall come to thy light, and kings to the brightness of thy rising.' (Isaiah 60.3).

It may be true, I think it is true, that in large measure we only come to the light of life provided by faith in God when 'other helpers fail and comforts flee'. And it may well be that we shall see this return to faith in our time when we are wearied in our modern world with the twilight of the alternative gods that we have set up. In any case this is the strong, upholding message of this season; the light which is God, the true God, is always there, always available, it can always be a source of life.

'When other helpers fail and comforts flee,
Help of the helpless, O abide with me.'

(H. F. Lyte, 1847)

Why do we come back? For one straight reason, we must have light. No plant, no animal, no human, can exist for long wholly without light. Light means life. Darkness means death. Which is why in the end the 'Gentiles' (that is, outsiders) 'shall come to thy light, and kings' (that is, 'top-people') 'to the brightness of thy rising.' Men will not, cannot for ever leave God out.

All this, of course, is pictorially presented at Epiphany in the story of the Wise Men guided by a star to the infant Christ. They were outsiders and they came. They were 'top-people' and they made the journey. And they were guided by a very small light, the shining of a star that can only be seen when the sky is dark.

Perhaps this is not only dramatic representation? Perhaps it is historical, or at least has a historical basis? Whatever we decide, the story of the Wise Men following a star is true to life. God rarely floods our path with light, he only gives sufficient for the step ahead.

At the beginning of *Pilgrim's Progress* is this telling incident. Evangelist was pointing with his finger across a wide field, and then addressed the pilgrim. 'Do you see yonder wicket-gate?' And he replied, 'No'. Then he said, 'Do you see yonder shining light?' He said, 'I think I do.' Then said Evangelist, 'Keep that light in your eye and go up directly thereto, so shalt thou see the gate.'

I think I am sufficiently old to testify that God rarely gives sufficient light to let us see the way across the entire field. He only grants sufficient light for the next step, and when we have taken that, for the one that follows.

'Lead kindly light, amid the encircling gloom,
Lead thou me on.
The night is dark, and I am far from home,
Lead thou me on.
Keep thou my feet, I do not ask to see
The distant scene; one step enough for me.'

(J. H. Newman)

And so the Epiphany message is very simple but very compelling. Do not discard the light of faith in God because we experience it as something very small. Do not let people argue you out of your faith because it does not solve *all* the world's problems. Do not talk to people, do not preach to people, as if all the fields of human experience and difficulty will be flooded with light if we adopt the Christian faith. That is not true, and it does not help to exaggerate what is. 'Thou also shalt light *my candle:* the Lord my God shall make my darkness to be light.' It is only a candle, only a small light, but without even a candle, still available and usable when all the great substitutes have failed, how very dark it is!

My friends, do not reject the candle.

EPIPHANY

Christ the disclosure man

Matthew 8.27 (NEB) '*What sort of man is this? Even the wind and the sea obey him*'

Some time ago one of our M.P.s wrote to one of the daily papers a letter in which he said he thought he knew what the Church's basic belief was; it could be summed up in a hymn of which he was particularly fond:

'The Church's one foundation
Is Jesus Christ her Lord.'

(S. J. Stone 1839-1900)

But as a result of all the sermons he had recently heard he was beginning to wonder. Was it perhaps 'the arms for South Africa' issue? Or aid for the under-developed countries? Or more social benefits at home?

1. *Socio-political activism or pietism?*

I know I am on dangerous ground. There are some people

who would like all Church life to consist of sociological and political activity. They equate this with Christianity and they cannot see much sense in churches unless they are constantly campaigning for some improvement in man's environment.

Over against them there are others who would opt for keeping out of all political and social concerns altogether, concentrating on the cultivation of an inner spiritual life. This view is usually associated with what is called 'pietism' and the wrongness of it is often indicated by a reference to pre-war Germany where in many cases the things of God and the affairs of State were so kept in water-tight compartments that it was possible for good churchmen to turn blind eyes to the monstrosities the State was perpetrating.

So what shall we decide in this issue? Is the Church to give priority to sociological and political activity? Or is it to give an absolute priority to the cultivation of the inner spiritual life?

2. *The Christ of the New Testament*

Neither of these views is correct. The first necessity for the Church is to cause men and women to see what Jesus Christ is like and then to present that Christ to the world, by all the ways open to it; which means words and deeds and lives, taking care all the time to see that the Christ presented really is the Christ of the New Testament and not some Christ of man's own wishful thinking.

Perhaps you do not follow what I mean so let me give two examples.

At the present time there are some Christian people so convinced that apartheid is wrong (and it is), and so convinced that it can never be done away with or modified by peaceful means that they are willing to finance guerrilla activities to overthrow violently the Government that supports it. And when asked how this can be squared with Christ they try to make out by long and tortuous arguments that actually Jesus was a secret supporter of the Zealot party in his day, devoted to the violent overthrow of the Romans. There is no substantial evidence for this reading the Gospels. It represents twisting the narrative to bolster up preconceived views.

A second example of twisting is this. In reaction against anti-Semitism (which is an evil thing), some Christian scholars are trying to say that the Jews had no part at all in the crucifixion of Jesus. The villains in the piece were entirely the Romans. This is not true.

My point then is this, that the Church's first responsibility is to see to it that Christ is made available to the world, the Christ of the New Testament. This does not mean sociological and political involvement is necessarily out. It does not mean that a deep concern with the inner spiritual life is out. What is at issue is a question of priorities. The Church must let Christ be seen and he must be the Christ of the New Testament.

3. *Who is Christ?*

And so the question raises its head again. What or who is the Christ of the New Testament? It is the question the Gospel for today (Epiphany IV), brings to our notice. Let me recall the occasion. Twelve men in a boat, twelve men who had spent their lives handling boats, on the lake of Galilee, but this time everything was beyond their power; the winds and the sea were about to swallow them up. And their passenger, Jesus, was asleep in the boat. And when they woke him, protesting their plight, he rebuked them for their fearfulness and immediately stilled the storm with a word. No wonder they gasped 'What sort of man is this, that even the wind and the sea obey him?' And that still is our question, the question we and every generation has to face for itself if it would possess *Christian* faith. What sort of man is this? How are we to understand this Christ?

First I want to say with all the emphasis I can that Jesus was a real man. In the boat he was fast asleep. Why? Because he was tired! Or again, when he was confronted with five thousand people to feed he asked the disciples how many loaves they had. Why? Because he did not know. Or again, when he knelt in the garden of Gethsemane the night before his crucifixion, his flesh quivered in anguish. Why? Because it was real flesh sensing what a flogging would do and what nails would do! We must have it firmly fixed in our minds that Jesus was a real man, with all the attractions and limitations of being a man. He was not God masquerading or dressed up *like a man.*

Secondly we must hold firmly to the belief that Jesus was not simply a man like one of us only a bit better. In him God's life was being lived out. In him the Transcendent was brought into our own limited mode of human existence, not only of environment, so that Jesus had to wash, eat breakfast, acquire information and rest like every other man, but he entered human flesh. The technical word is 'Incarnation'. What this means is that Jesus in himself is *the disclosure point of God in man.*

At the present time there is a tendency in some quarters to run away from this and to imagine that Christianity will survive, even flourish, if we assert that Jesus was simply a super-compassionate man for others. But there is nothing distinctive about our faith and no gospel exists in it unless we are prepared to proclaim that at this point in history, namely in Jesus of Nazareth, that other level of being, the Transcendent, the Supernatural, the 'Other' (call it what you will), was being made visible and available in a man.

4. *Our order of priorities*

So we come back to the hymn the M.P. loved so well and wrote to the paper about:

> 'The Church's one foundation
> Is Jesus Christ her Lord'

It is the Church's first task to let that Christ be seen, to encourage people to come into our churches and other places of quiet, to get him into focus, to worship him and to pray to God through him. And to go out into the cloud and the sunshine to live him out ourselves in whatever ways and places are appropriate for us. I am confident that this order of priorities is of fundamental importance. At the top we must put Christ, the man who lived God (as Bishop Barry expressed it); next we must come away from the world to meet him.

Thirdly we must go out and about among men living out the new kind of Christ-like life that has been given us. This is the order of priorities. This is the pattern that makes for balanced and wholesome Christian witness. Christ is the disclosure man.

THE CONVERSION OF ST PAUL

Our debt to St Paul

On the back page of a newspaper supplement recently there was an advertisement for two books, which purported to give an insight into the minds of one hundred great thinkers, men who changed the world by their ideas. In the list were the names Julius Caesar, Leonardo da Vinci, Voltaire and Lenin and also the name of the man January 25 commemorates, Saul of Tarsus, or as he is better known, St Paul.

The world was never the same after St Paul came. This ought to give us some idea of the size of his thinking. To look at he was not all that distinguished. He was short in stature, bow-legged, blue-eyed and subject to a recurring illness very like epilepsy. But in every other way he was an outsize man, with a massive intellect, massive will-power, massive strength to endure. One minute you could count him a lawyer, the next minute a poet, then all at once he turns into an organizer. It is impossible to get tabs on Paul. He stands in a class by himself. He belongs to the category of genius, and that at times seems almost akin to madness. So he seemed to Festus when he cried out to his prisoner 'Paul, thou art mad! thy much learning doth turn thee to madness.' But you had to take note of Paul. The whole world has had to take note of Paul. No situation, place or person was quite the same after Paul had made his contact.

But why is he important? What debt do we owe him now? Let us be practical.

1. *His letters*

First, he wrote a large part of the New Testament. Not with his own hand, of course. He couldn't. His eyes were too weak. But he dictated letters to a scribe and then signed them with his own rather large handwriting. 'The salutation of me, Paul, with my own hand', and then the huge characters PAUL. Most of those letters came from prison. It isn't easy to write in prison, especially if you are handcuffed to a soldier. I wonder sometimes if we stop to think of the dungeons from which much of our New Testament comes. And the letters were written under pressure, under pressure of events, problems and situations that were getting out of hand. Paul's writing is not for the most part the cool, detached writing of a philosopher, but hot, urgent and involved. Sentences spill over into each other, trains of thought are started, only to break off into others. It is very hard to catch up with Paul. He is always in a hurry, always thinking on to the next subject. Yes, we are indebted to Paul for much of the dynamic writing of the New Testament that has never ceased to catch fire in the minds of other men.

2. *His abolition of 'religion'*

Secondly, however, it is what he did about religion that makes him most important. In a sense he abolished it. And a statement like that is easy to misunderstand, just as Bonhoeffer nowadays is often misunderstood, because he spoke in terms like this. But what he said doesn't mean the abolition of prayer and worship and godly living. It means the abolition of all ideas of religious merit. You see, Saul of Tarsus, to call him by his former name, had been through all that. He had kept the commandments. He had been a rigorist in synagogue attendance. His pedigree was unimpeachable. He had a passion for right living—but it got him nowhere, except into pride, fanaticism and heresy hunting, the very antithesis of justice. And so he threw it all away, every reliance on personal achievement, every assurance based on his own supposed moral rectitude, he cast on to the refuse heap. Nothing we can do commends us to God, he said, nothing at all, our only commendation is that Christ died and rose again for us, something outside us.

And of course that is revolutionary. It turned the moral thinking of men and women upside down. Because since the world began people do think they can run up a credit account with God—self-denial, large donations, small donations, works of mercy, even church-going, even coming to the Holy Communion, God has a ledger and enters up the things we do, and when our day comes and we knock on the gate, the final gate, out will come that ledger and then we'll know the worst or best, according as our merit stands.

St Paul scrapped the entire notion. No ledger book exists, and even if it did, no entries made would ever make the slightest difference. On those terms no-one would ever enter through the gate at all. No-one would ever come into the divine presence.

So what is the way? Why is Paul important? Because he showed the world the magnitude of 'the Christ event', the towering majesty of what Christ had done, namely (to use the words of the Te Deum, the Christian Hymn) 'he opened the kingdom of heaven to all believers'.

You and I haven't begun our A B C of the Christian Gospel, the Christian good news, unless we have got hold of this. We men and women never go up one by one to knock at God's door, offering our credit cards of good deeds done and bad deeds avoided, and hoping or bargaining for an entry. The whole door has gone, door posts, lintel, step—the lot. Christ has removed it. 'He has opened the kingdom of heaven to all believers.' So the way in to God now, tomorrow, next week and when we die is not by merit but by faith, faith in Christ, our representative. It is in him we trust.

3. *A faith for all men*

And so it is that St Paul has done two great things for the world. He has lifted Jesus Christ out from his setting in Judaism and placed him down among the peoples of the world, making Christianity a world religion, open to everybody of whatever race or class or economic background.

And secondly, he has shown us what is the right response to Christ, not straining ourselves up to copy his standard, but thanking him in heart and mind for what he has done. This puts us on his side, it means our heart goes along with his. So we believe in him. And it is this which brings us home to God.

Simple? Yes. Very simple, but profound. And revolutionary. It is summed up in the words from Ephesians 2.8 (NEB). 'For it is by his grace you are saved, through trusting him; it is not your own doing. It is God's gift, not a reward for work done. There is nothing for any one to boast of.'

SEPTUAGESIMA

Knowing the giver

INTRODUCTION

I would like you to imagine for a moment that there is a ring at the door of your flat. You are not expecting a caller but when you answer the bell a cardboard box is handed in to you. Surprised, you close the door and begin examining the parcel. You deal with the Sellotape, your patience tried, then with the white tissue paper, then the contents. You are quite overcome. A superb piece of clothing from one of the best business houses in Knightsbridge is packed inside. But quickly your thrill fades. You do not know the giver. It is true there is a card in the box and it bears a man's name. But you do not know him. You can't remember ever having seen him. So why the present? Could there be a trick in this? Is something being 'tried on' to get you in a corner? So you rewrap the parcel, stuff it in a drawer and wonder what to do.

Now let me tell a second story. There is a ring at the door

of your flat. You are not expecting a caller but when you answer the bell a cardboard box is handed in. Surprised, you examine the parcel. There is the Sellotape to deal with and the white tissue paper. And then inside you find a quite superb piece of clothing from one of the best business houses in Knightsbridge. And there on the top of the garment a small white card which says 'With love from Mary'. At which your heart is lifted up. You could almost dance across the room. A beautiful present from Mary. You do not stuff that garment away in a drawer; you wear it next day and feel twice as good for doing so. It is a wonderful gift that warms your heart.

Now my question. So simple, yet in a way so profound. Why is the present enjoyed in the second case and not in the first? After all, it was the same present, delivered in the same way, with the same Sellotape and the same white tissue paper. The answer is, because in the second case *the recipient knew the donor.*

1. *God the Creator*

This is Septuagesima Sunday, the day when traditionally we give our minds to a fundamental Christian doctrine, the doctrine of God as creator of the world; when we read that magnificent opening chapter of the Bible, 'In the beginning God created the heaven and the earth'. And the opening chapter of St. John's Gospel, 'In the beginning was the Word, and the Word was with God, and the Word was God. . . . All things were made by him; and without him was not anything made that was made'. This Sunday we look out in imagination on the giant universe, the planets, the stars, the Milky Way, the moon and the earth; and on the earth mountains and hills, the valleys and rivers, the trees, the colours, the shadows, the streams, the flowers, all the rich variety of the natural order; a magnificent present all on our doorstep and we tear the Sellotape (as it were), and unwrap the white tissue paper. . . and what is the result? Well? Everything by way of lasting reaction depends on whether or not we really *know the giver.*

In some people's view, of course, let us face it, there is no giver. The universe just arrived or just is. This will not be the view of most people and it will not be our view as churchgoers. We shall see the universe, we shall see the world and nature as God's creation, God's gift. And we may reckon that to be a satisfactory and satisfying religious concept by itself, but I do not think so. In order to enjoy a present we need to *know the giver*. We need to know the character of the one responsible for the gift.

All this is so because the Creator's gift of the universe and of the world of nature has many baffling aspects to it. Nowadays with our scientific advancement we are more conscious of the harsh aspects of the created order than were Longfellow, Wordsworth and Tennyson who waxed lyrical over the loveliness they saw. That loveliness is still there, but what a tiny strip of the universe holds it. Go fifteen miles up and your blood would boil. Go fifteen miles down and you would not survive a minute. There is only a very thin layer of atmosphere around our globe which makes possible the loveliness we humans know. The rest is harsh and bare and majestic and silent. We need only think for a moment of what we know of the face of the moon. Over against all this, how can *I* count, a tiny speck on the oceans of time and that speck dogged by accidents, illnesses, diseases, sorrows, frustrations, disappointments and death.

Sometimes we meet people as we go about who say 'God as Creator is good enough for me, the God of the hills and the sky and the daffodils in the park, each one a thing of beauty in itself. Why all this talk about sin and redemption, of reconciliation and atonement, of a Cross and resurrection the third day? It is all so unnecessary isn't it?' But when your heart is really broken, does it help at all to go out and look at the stars? When you are up against it, not knowing what decision to make, are you really strengthened by a sight of a carpet of bluebells? If I know anything about these experiences at all the only outcome from gazing at this loveliness is an increase in sadness. 'Oh, if only the whole of life was such as this. Why must we have these frightful upsets?'

This is my point this morning. We shall not greatly benefit by the gift unless we *know the giver* apart from his gift.

2. *Christ the revealer*

And so on this Sunday we have it brought home to us that not only do we need God the Creator, not only do we need a world of beautiful things and useful things and remarkable things, every one of them material, we need to know the God who gave them and that is possible through Jesus Christ.

It is a fine thing that I can contemplate God as the maker of the Pleiades and Orion, but it is a much more helpful thing to see Christ take little children in his arms, running noses and all, and bless them every one. It is a noble aspiration to conceive of the Architect of a world who counts it worth while to make a dragon-fly in the most glorious colours destined to live for twenty-four hours and nothing more beyond. But it is more empowering to me to see that same Lord in Jesus Christ restoring the sight of some blind beggar to whom no one gave a moment's thought.

I hope all of us here believe in God the Creator. 'In the beginning God created the heaven and the earth', Genesis chapter one verse one, my text for this morning. But I hope we trust him all the more for this, that 'God so loved the world, that he gave his only begotten Son, that whosoever believeth in him should not perish but have eternal life.'

3. *Christian joy*

Then the gifts of God will make us happy because we *know the giver*. Those blackbirds which find it possible to sing even in this built-up area will make us glad, so will the yellow sky at dawn and the first signs of almond blossom in the gardens round about. These things should make us glad. We should as Christians rejoice in all and every kind of natural beauty and all the lovely things of life more than the rest, for this one reason, that in Jesus Christ we know the great eternal giver, God, Creator of the earth and heaven.

SEXAGESIMA

Two gardens

Almost every Englishman loves a garden, and it is about two gardens I would like you to think today. In our big cities a garden almost plays the part of Paradise, an oasis of greenness in a wilderness of concrete. In the Middle East, too, a garden is almost a heavenly thing. Think what it means to jog day after day upon a camel's back across some barren, scorching desert, where the sandy wastes seem never to end. But the traveller reaches a garden, a pool of water, a patch of green, a plantation of trees, a seat, shade—and if there is a gardener—even some flowers. Is it any wonder God has always been associated with gardens and the devil has always been associated with wasteland?

1. *Rebellion in a garden*

And so we need not be surprised that on page two (so to speak) of the Bible we are introduced to a garden, a large garden, set out with trees, well-watered and brim-full with life. What catches the eye, however, is a woman in conversation with a snake. And until yesterday in modern times it all seemed so silly because snakes do not speak. But now even technological man must see that life cannot be all squeezed within the confines of scientific measurement. An irrational element exists that we neglect at our peril. Of course snakes do not speak, but somehow the writer of Genesis intended to communicate the point that the idea of rebelling against God was suggested to the mind of man by *something in God's created order*. After all, God created the snake, and God created the matter that makes for materialism!

Note that mankind is represented by a woman; and the snake is dubbed 'subtle' and so it is. It begins by asking if God has really prohibited man from eating of all the trees in the garden. A silly question, but useful. After all, why have an orchard if you cannot eat the apples! Why have sexual instincts if we cannot freely indulge them? But the silly question serves its purpose. The woman corrects the snake, *but in doing so she exaggerates.* God had never said they weren't to *touch* the tree. This is the woman's addition. And exaggeration means weakness. And the snake knows it, which is why it already has this woman on the run. Its next remark is not silly but blatant. God's commands are not for man's good but for his own status. That is to say, God may be powerful, but he is not good. This is a criticism of God, a criticism as old as the hills. And the woman falls for it. It could be that *man* knows best what is good for man, and not God! It could be that man should be the master of his own destiny! It could be advantageous for man's development to acknowledge no power over his life whatsoever, no power that is beyond himself, the kind of viewpoint the Provost of King's, Cambridge, teaches. Nothing beyond man. Humanism triumphant. Humanism regnant. Then he will develop his senses, his culture and his learning. So you see the woman's eye in the garden widening. The fruit of the forbidden tree was good for food, pleasant to the eye and to be desired to make one wise.

But why a woman to represent mankind? Why Eve? Why not Adam? Because when it comes to subtle questions about life, woman, by reason of her intuition, is there before the man. Adam was probably turning the compost heap or sowing seeds; just as on Sunday mornings the men are tinkering with the car while their wives are in church worshipping. The man arrives in time, of course. And when he arrives he often outstrips the woman both in reflection on mystical questions *and* in rebellion. That is his nature. But if you stay sufficiently long staring into the garden, you will see them both rebellious, and both dishonoured, Adam and Eve, each in each other's presence, till they have to quit the garden, a painful scene, quitting a place they themselves have planted, and every flower they have grown to love—and not only the garden, but God *in the garden.* Don't miss that point. All this is in the story of Adam and Eve in the garden of Eden, and more, a rebellion in *a lovely place*. And that today we know is true, because it is in the affluent society where men are not poor, or ill-clothed or hungry, that they have given up belief in God.

2. *Obedience in a garden*

And now let us look at the other garden, not a mythical garden this time, but a garden you could find on a map. It was a city garden, or at least, a garden close to a city wall, so it was an oasis of a kind, a place of peace and meditation. And quite often if you looked into that garden you would see a man sitting, the man whom St Paul, in a flash of theological insight, called 'the second man', 'the last Adam', Jesus of Nazareth. The fourth Gospel tells us that he often resorted to this garden, the garden of Gethsemane.

Now there came a Thursday night, when the moon was full, that he was there again. But not quietly this time. Now standing. Now kneeling. Clearly something terrible was agitating his soul. His whole frame quivered in an agony of reactionary sensation, and all because of the dawn to break so soon. And with the dawn would come the dragging tiredness, the flogging, the hot searing pain, the thirst, the mockery, the vulgar exhibition, the draining out of every drop of blood upon a jagged, wooden, Roman cross. And here in the garden was his last chance, a chance his disciples had already taken. They were over the wall by now. And he was young. He, too, could do the same. It was as easy as that. Ten thousand Galileans would hide him. Half an hour was left. Half an hour in which to obey what he knew to be the will of God for him, half an hour to temporize and finally escape. And you watch and I watch. Trembling we watch, till suddenly the garden gate gets thrust aside. Striding soldiers burst into the stillness. The Nazarene is there, still there, still in the garden. And he goes forward, you see him giving himself up. He did not think he knew a better way than God. He involved himself in no rebellion. That is what 'the second Adam' did in a garden. Jesus the Christ obeyed God till his final draught of breath.

3. *A garden not enough*

Two gardens—one in a story, one in history, one in Eden, one in Gethsemane. I do not think we shall be interested in the second, unless we receive the message of the first. If our philosophy is that all man requires for his progress is a better environment, more amenities, higher wages, more education, in other words, a bigger and better garden (I said all), then of course any kind of Christ is irrelevant. But if the Genesis diagnosis is correct, that is to say if the life of man has within it the seeds of its own failure, however perfect the environment, then some spiritual Saviour is needed in addition to material benefits. And this the second garden offers. It offers Jesus the Christ man, the man for others, the man for us, who will stay with us, suffer for us, rise from the dead for us. And that resurrection took place in a garden, too.

Today is Sexagesima Sunday, the day when we think of the Fall of Man, as it is called, not something historical, but something contemporary. Man *is* a fallen creature. But it need not be a sad day. It can be a joyous day, for we have not been left to our own devices. There is a power to lift us up, a transcendent power made available in Christ, made available through faith, made available by trust, the very reversal of rebellion. It is what society desperately needs today. It needs contact with the Divine to lift it up. Please God this is what our worship in Church offers, not merely a traditional ritual which can be empty, but a means of contact with the living God, who takes us, and sometimes breaks and then remakes us after his image. This is real religion. It is the thing in which I passionately believe. . . .

QUINQUAGESIMA

The vision of the vertical

Genesis 12.9 (RSV) *'And Abram journeyed on still going toward the Negeb.'*

I guess people laughed at him. Unless I am absolutely wrong about Sarai his wife—that ravishingly beautiful woman—there were times when she mocked at him too. And of an evening back in Ur in Chaldea, when the sun went down and the wine was poured from golden flagons, and the guests were arrayed in flowing silken robes, the wealthy burghers laughed about their former fellow citizen, Abram the visionary. 'Good for him if he wants to be for ever on the road! Good for him if a tent and goat's milk are all he fancies!' And could you have seen him then, and could I have seen him then, we too might have wondered. The Negeb lay ahead of him. You can find it on the map if you have the patience. The Negeb, a frightening waste of desert land and rocks, where nothing grows and human life for ever hangs upon a thread. Are you surprised that back in the fertile crescent they laughed at him for going there? 'And Abram journeyed on, still going toward the Negeb.'

I want to talk to you today about seeing life as a journey, a pilgrimage, a trek upon a road, the end of which you cannot clearly see. Ever since the world began and men have thought about our human life there has been this picture of a journey. Vergil's *Aeneid*, Dante's *Divine Comedy*, Bunyan's *Pilgrim's Progress*, Pasternak's *Dr. Zhivago*, with its trans-Siberian railroad. Yes, and at another level, the old First World War song of the troops:

'There's a long, long trail a-winding. . . .'

And Harry Lauder singing:

'Keep right on to the end of the road,
Keep right on to the end.'

1. *Horizontal living*

You ask me who Abram is and I'll tell you. Abram is the father of all those people who are not satisfied with life as a thing of *horizontal dimensions*. Perhaps there are three forms in which this most commonly appears.

First, life seen as a preoccupation with money. At one end of the social scale, endless wage demands. At the other end the readiness to knock down anything of beauty, age or usefulness, if the result can be a rise in income. Life is for money-making. But the end that way is boredom. We go to work to earn the money to buy the food to make us strong to go to work to earn the money. . . . I call that horizontal living, the end of which is stark futility.

Second, life interpreted as pleasure-hunting. And of course the view is understandable. No-one who has ever seen people engaged on modern production lines, no-one who has ever known what it feels like to be tied to a routine (in which you are no kind of master), is ever going to make light of what it means to be out and away to the seaside in a car with every road a possibility. I understand the modern pathetic absorption with the motor car. It offers man a break from routine where freedom to decide is given back again. *But* pleasure-hunting by itself alone is apt to pall with great rapidity. I only need to ask the question, 'Are there any pictures more depressing than the faces of those poor rich people with nothing to do but fill up time on endless pleasure cruises in the Caribbean?'

A *third* example of horizontal living which does not satisfy has gripped us in the West with terrifying tightness. It is the idea that nothing is real that cannot be measured, nothing is real that cannot be weighed, nothing is real that is not subject to forecasting calculation. Everything is explicable. There is no *in*explicable. This means not only is there no God, there is no man, that is to say, no man who is other than a highly complicated machine, able to be analysed, able to be conditioned, a temporal tool for the community's benefit, with no eternal part or destiny. That is what we have come to—mechanical determinism.

And all around, of course, are protests by the young, pathetic protests, useless protests, the kind of protest made by D. H. Lawrence against the mechanization which he saw in the Midlands. The way out is sought through the senses, through the uninhibited play of every sexual instinct; and now the entry into fantasy with the aid of various drugs. All this is a revolt from horizontal living (which is no life at all), grasping at the only kind of spiritual things a godless age can countenance, erotic love and chemically induced emotion.

2. *Vertical living*

What man needs to be man is a *vertical dimension*. What man needs to lift him up from his mechanistic bondage is a spiritual illumination. This is the significance of Abram. This is what it means to live our life as on a journey. We are not stuck in grim determinism. We are not only dust and clay reverting in the end to dust and clay. Man has a spirit. And you cannot tape it, you cannot calculate it, you cannot analyse it, and you cannot bring it into being. The spirit of man has the possibility of an eternal destiny. His road, his journey from the womb *goes somewhere*. You may laugh because we cannot tell you where exactly, but out there beyond the gate of material disintegration there is something great and wonderful, the positive of every negative we experience now.

A few days ago we spent an unforgettable evening at Covent Garden watching and hearing Beethoven's only opera *Fidelio*. In the middle of that opera there occurs a scene which must be one of the most moving on any stage at any time, the 'Chorus of the Prisoners'. Out from their darkened, cramping cells creep forty or so men in filthy rags. They find it hard to stand up straight, and even harder still to bear the light outside. And then they sing a muted harmony pouring out the pathos of their prison plight.

And that, if they knew, was the cramped and darkened life of the citizens of Ur who laughed at Abram. And that, too, is the cramped and darkened life of every kind of horizontal living, be it money-making, pleasure seeking, or mechanical interpretation of what a man is. But Abram made the break. He responded to a vision he could not explain. He went after that vision he could never reach. He quitted Ur and he took to the road. Life for him would be a pilgrimage to the eternal city. 'And Abram journeyed on still going toward the Negeb. . . . He looked for the city. . . whose builder and maker is God.' That is what made him a man, a leader of men, the father of all the men of faith who have ever lived who do not walk merely by sight.

3. *The work of Christ*

And Christ took that road. He did not know, but he trusted that at the end there was a gate into the Father's presence. And for our sake he rose again *to give our vision substance*, the vision of the vertical, lest we fall back to horizontal living and become a pigmy people.

LENT

The mixture

> Luke 11.13 (NEB) '*If you, then, bad as you are, know how to give your children what is good for them, how much more will the heavenly Father give the Holy Spirit to those who ask him!*'

I don't want to appear irreverent nor in any way to cheapen this verse of scripture, but I think I should have to describe it as a bit of a 'backhander'.

1. *The badness in the mixture*

But you ask, 'Who said it and to whom?' And the answer is, our Lord said it to his disciples when he was talking to them about prayer. 'If you, then, bad as you are. . . .' How would you take that? How did the disciples take it? The phrase is slipped in almost before you are aware of it, and before you have time to reply or protest. It is presented as if this interpretation of man is axiomatic. Man is bad, even disciples are bad, even disciples enquiring about prayer and receiving a first lesson in which the Lord's Prayer was incorporated. They are bad. Everyone is bad. 'If you, then, bad as you are. . . .' This is the testimony of Jesus about people, people in general.

And our hackles rise. We begin to splutter. 'Look' we say, 'look at all the good things we do. Look at our Welfare. Look at our contribution to underdeveloped countries. Look at the improvement in the lot of the poor in this country these last hundred years. You don't see children with rickets today, nor tramps wrapped up in newspaper on the Embankment seats. There are no hunger marches.'

But it seems silly to list all these beneficial actions because our Lord does it for us in the same breath. 'If you, then, bad as you are, know how to give your children what is good for them. . . .' All our protest is there in the words of Jesus himself.

This is our trouble, isn't it? I mean the trouble of the last twenty-five years (and more, of course). We won't face up to the duplicity of man. Has there ever been such a colossal misreading in our time? Give people more money, better homes, higher standards of living, then stealing and violence and law-breaking and beastliness will decline because there won't be any incentives to evil. Put people in a good environment and they will become good. It all sounds so easy and people still believe it, contrary to the glaring facts of the last twenty-five years.

The harsh truth about man is that he is a twister, twisting whatever circumstances prevail, be they good or bad, to turn them to his own advantage, even if other people, old or young, infirm or healthy, suffer in consequence. The Welfare State is largely in the muddle it is today for not recognizing that basic fact. People will abuse the welfare designed to help them.

2. *The good in the mixture*

That is one side of the picture—and now the other. 'If you,

then. . . know how to give your children what is good for them.' If the disciples, if we, had not been smarting over the first phrase, slipped in as a back-hander, we would be smiling contentedly over this bit, 'we know how to give our children what is good for them.' That is the estimate of the Christ himself about us human beings. What a fine lot we are, intelligent, discerning, kindly, generous!

And this is also true. If I didn't know it before, I knew it in my early forties when I did a considerable amount of religious broadcasting. The generosity of the British public on behalf of anyone distressed, unfortunate, suffering or under-privileged, and this extends to children and animals, is quite amazing.

I shall not easily forget in my second year in this church, how I said in a broadcast that I lived in a city far away from the open countryside, the flowers and the birds. That did it. All the following week bunches of flowers and leaves, even damp moss in a cardboard box, which I was told to smell because it would remind me of the country, arrived through the post. And to crown all, a woman from Ireland arrived on my doorstep, offering me the free loan of a bungalow for a fortnight on the coast of Ireland so that I could see that lovely place for myself.

That is the other truth about people, a very real and genuine goodness, too. So what is the proper estimate to make of human nature? It is neither pessimistic, nor optimistic; instead, it is realist. Human nature is a mixture of good and bad, and the endless problem is which side is going to win.

Jesus said 'If you, then, bad as you are, know how to give your children what is good for them, how much more will the heavenly Father give the Holy Spirit to those who ask him.' And that is the point. The good part in man needs reinforcement to overcome the evil part. The human spirit needs the divine Spirit. It needs it if there is to be victory in the conflict.

3. *Reinforcement by asking*

But how does this come about? How does a man, how does a community obtain the help of the Spirit of God?

And it is all so simple. We can scarcely believe it. Merely by asking! 'How much more will the heavenly Father give the Holy Spirit to those *who ask him*!'

But asking is often our problem. It means putting our pride in our pocket. It means confessing that we are not self-sufficient on our own. It means admitting that our intelligence is not the final answer to all our problems, social and personal. We are not all that strong. But God is gracious. Ask and we shall receive, seek and we shall find. Knock, and the door will be opened. So said Christ in the context of our verse.

The best thing for our country today would be to get down on our knees again and confess that for all our goodness we are miserable (that means wretched) sinners, standing in need of God's reinforcing Spirit; we could have it and win, if only we would own up and ask.

LENT

A hostile setting

1. *A siege* (Luke 22.1-23)

Here are two men standing in a street doorway. It was not a South Kensington street, but more like a street in the City of London, say Bread Street or Carter Lane, if you know them—narrow, winding and closed in with high buildings. The alleyways called 'Calle' in Venice would be a better parallel. The time is evening. It is dark, but not quite dark, having just enough light and just enough dark to make the time eerie. You encounter people before you really see them. And that is best for these two men in the doorway. Truth to tell, they are afraid. They sense something. But they have a duty to perform. They have to keep their eyes open for a man displaying an identification mark. They are involved in a plan not knowing all the clues.

All at once they see him, the man they are looking for.

They do not speak. They nudge each other and follow him. He doesn't turn round, nor do they accost him. Yet they feel he knows they are there. Somehow they sense it. On his head he is carrying a jar of water, steadying it with his hand. Abruptly he stops and knocks on a doorway. Almost without a pause the door is opened. This is the moment for the two men following. Is it safe? Could this be a trap? But they must take their chance. With swift steps they hurry forward to address the householder with the phrase they have repeated a hundred times to get it right. 'The Master says "Where is the room in which I may eat the Passover with my disciples?" ' It sounded innocuous enough. Hundreds of other strangers would be asking the same question that night. No-one overhearing would raise an eyebrow. So the plan succeeds. They are shown a large room upstairs all set out for an evening meal, obviously the best room. They had expected something different, something humbler on the ground floor. Obviously this householder is on their side. So they aren't afraid. They remain in the room completing the preparations.

Presently they hear a sound on the steps outside. So keyed up are they, they note every footfall. Then they breathe again. Jesus walks in. In fact his manner sets them at ease. Ten men follow him.

In due course the meal begins. Thirteen at the table. Tension rises. For one thing, there had been an undignified scramble for the best seats, and a sense of hurt for the rebukes that followed. But what really unsettles them is the sudden realization that the enemy isn't in the street outside, but actually at the table. Jesus says 'The hand that betrays me is on the table now'.

Then, as if what had happened was not enough, Jesus announces that this is his last meal. His words make the air heavy. All the foundations of their lives seem out of joint. Yet, as if there were all the time in the world and their ways were stabilized on rock foundations, quietly Jesus takes a piece of bread, breaks it into pieces, and distributes it among the twelve. He does the same with a cup of wine after he has given thanks and blessed it. Every man in the room takes the bread, every man sips the cup, the enemy in the room among them.

Unexpectedly (everything is unexpected), Jesus serves the choicest portion of the supper dish to the man closest to him. It represents a gesture to an honoured guest which invariably warmed his heart, winning over even the hostile. But not tonight. Having received the token, the favoured man makes for the door and opens it. Every eye follows his every movement. And as they do so, momentarily they notice something, they notice how dark is the night. Then the door is closed. Footsteps descend the stone stairway and die away, the footsteps of Judas, the man from Kerioth.

2. *A sacrament*

This story is to be continued, but first notice one fact in the part already told. The Holy Communion was instituted almost under siege conditions. In old Jerusalem that night with its narrow streets, its dark and crooked corners, the foes of Jesus were gathering in. They were only waiting for one thing, the opportunity to strike, and they knew it would come that night, Thursday night, because Judas, one of the twelve, had been willing to receive money to betray him.

Why was the Holy Communion instituted? Look back to that night. It was to keep those twelve men together. The attempt was even made by means of it to keep Judas in the group. But with him it failed. The purpose, however, was clear. It was to be a bond of union. Especially after Jesus' departure it was meant to be an unifying instrument. That is why he said 'Do this in remembrance of me'.

3. *A bond of union*

I am not sure that the Church has obeyed Christ altogether over the Holy Communion. It has in fact become the sharpest point of disunion, instead of the place of coming together. Sometimes it has been used as a whip to try to get the unruly to toe the party line.

And sometimes it almost seems as if the original solemnity

is being taken out of the Holy Communion, and it is like to become a religious parish party with parts for everyone to play and lines to speak.

The Holy Communion is the meeting point of many deep and subtle doctrines, most of which would have been above the heads of the original twelve communicants. Its depth cannot be gainsaid and must not be forgotten, least of all that it is a Eucharist, a thanksgiving.

But let us not lose sight of the fact that the prime concern of the first participants was of the enemy without and within the gates.

Do not be surprised today if at any time almost the whole city casts hostile eyes upon the Church. The Holy Communion belonged originally to that kind of setting. It is not the whole story but it is part of it, a part we shall be wise to remember today. Christ provided for hostility. He gave us the Holy Communion to keep us together.

LENT

The test

1. *The Lord's test* (Luke 22.24-46)

We continue the story. It was broken off abruptly with the footfalls of a man descending a stone stairway and dissolving into silence along the street. We are not going to follow him. No-one followed him. We are going to wait outside in the street, that narrow, tortuous street, hemmed in by tall buildings. We are going to watch that stone stairway and the door at its summit.

We have to wait, and we suffer from the cold. But there is one satisfaction, the darkness lessens. Not because of the dawn's breaking—that will be at some time to come—but because of the full moon rising high in the sky, lighting up, it is true, only part of the street, but enough for us to watch those steps and the doorway at the top.

All at once the door opens. We count the men who appear. One, two, three. . . . In all there are eleven, not twelve. Twelve men descend to the street.

They do not proceed to the upper part of the city, but make for a graduated pathway, that is to say a road with steps sufficiently wide to allow asses and even camels to pass up and down. A similar kind of roadway can be seen at Clovelly in North Devon. The twelve men descend by this till they reach a gateway through the city wall. This, though guarded, is open all night. Two of the twelve at least are carrying offensive weapons. They keep them well covered as they pass through the gate. No more in Northern Ireland today than in Jerusalem under the Romans was it wise to be caught with illicit arms.

But they pass safely through and make for a garden. It is several hundred yards away. It is called Gethsemane which means 'oil-press' probably because of a primitive contraption made for crushing olives, worked by a donkey attached to a wheel. The place is quiet but not deathly quiet. The brook Kedron, skirting it, tumbles noisily in spring over the boulders in its bed; and every so often the silence of the night is pierced by the sharp staccato Latin cries of the Roman sentries pacing the walls of the tower of Antonia near-by.

The twelve men stumble into the garden. They seem all in. Conversation is at a standstill. Their limbs appear to drop them onto the ground under the trees, and eight are scarcely screened by them than they are asleep, drunk with sleep. Four proceed further into the secrecy of the place. Then they break. Only one walks on. The three bidden to wait collapse, sunk down in hopeless slumber. The one is Jesus of Nazareth.

Still we watch. Presently we see a lone battle. We are all but ashamed to watch. Nevertheless we see Jesus all but broken up. He does not stand, Jewish fashion, to pray. He crouches, kneels down, crumples. Something invisible is on him, like a hideous nightmare, something terrible, disgusting, filthy. It is as if he is being handed some stinking cup, revolting to the taste. Great beads of sweat course down his face. And yet he does not break. He stands erect again, sufficiently erect, and returns to the sleeping three and the sleeping eight. 'Rise and pray' he said, 'that you may be spared the test.'

2. *The Christian's prayer*

All down the ages Christians have repeated that prayer, in Latin, in Greek, in French, in German, in Italian, in English. 'Lead us not into temptation', or as in the New English Bible, 'Do not bring us to the test'.

This is where we go wrong in our modern way of life; we think we can manage the tests of life quite easily. We are so sure of ourselves, of our mastery of the elements, our strong technology and the computers we have constructed; there is no situation we need to fear. We shall pass the tests. So away with all censorship. Let Mr Lennon display his pornographic pictures. Let our sons and daughters be surrounded by whatever they like, whatever we like, violence, dirt, easy abortion, the 'pill' for everyone who wants it. All this is life. It is stupid to pull down the shutters on any single part. Temptation is a silly word. Modern man will pass his tests.

But will he? Is this the measure of our pride? Surely the humbler way is wiser. 'Lead us not into temptation. Do not bring us to the test.' Who knows that faced with the easy way, the lower way, the sensual way, the selfish way, the crooked way, any of us might not fall? So do not bring us to the test. Lead us not into temptation. Give us grace to avoid the trial.

Christ came through his test. We call it his agony in the garden. Perhaps we have forgotten while we have been thinking about our modern, proud, permissive society, that we are still watching in the garden of the 'oil-press'. But of the original twelve in the garden, only one is left, the Christ himself. The other eleven have heard the tramp of soldiers' feet coming towards the garden the way they came. They have seen the flaming torches and caught a glimpse of the swords and cudgels. They knew what to expect, and if Peter did lunge out with a sword, soon he too, with the others, was over the garden wall. They failed their test.

You would think that no doubt could possibly exist as to which group it is that we belong; to Christ, bending but never breaking in his test, or the eleven, scrambling madly over the garden wall to escape.

Perhaps the great majority today escape over the wall to avoid saying 'no' when it comes to the test. There is a great retreat all along the line from making a stand over what is difficult, unpopular and traditional. We daren't say 'no' to anything. And if, perhaps, we may be inclined to count ourselves the great exception, it might be wise to look again at that garden of the olive-press. Whose is the face of that man leading the tramping soldiers with their swords and cudgels? We have seen it before. It is the face of the same man we saw at the Holy Communion in the room at the top of the stairs, the face of the man from Kerioth, one of the apostles. Apparently even such can betray his Lord. And so we pray 'Lord, lead us not into temptation. Do not put us to the test.' We are so very frail.

LENT

The mockers

> Jude 18 (NEB) '*In the final age there will be men who pour scorn on religion, and follow their own godless lusts.*'

In a sense, of course, every age is the final age for the men living in it. The end of the world has already come for the generations that are past, and the end of the world is upon us now for those of us who are alive. We ought not therefore to postpone the warning of the apostles of Christ repeated in the short letter of Jude in the New Testament about the appearance of the mockers. Mockers of Christ will appear in every age. They are present now. One of the fashionable pastimes today is to lampoon religion. Some religion deserves it. Some forms of church life invite it. Some clergy ask for it. But the modern mockery does not only have its origin in the defects of the Christians, but also in the defects of the mockers. I will show you.

Thirteen times over the verb 'to mock' occurs in the New Testament, and eleven of those references have Christ as their object. Mockery was part of Christ's experience. Not in the days when men hung upon his words; not in the days when ill people crowded round for the touch of his healing hand or the sound of his exorcizing voice; the mockery came when he was caught. That is to say, men tied Christ up and then laughed at him; or they dressed him up in comic clothes—the soldier's red robe, the crown of thorns and the reed for a sceptre—and then they mocked. It was rather like boys baiting an animal. First they make sure that it is reduced to impotence and then they prod it with sticks and knives.

1. *Christ's mockers*

As far as I can discover, there were five sets of mockers during the passion of our Lord.

First, there were the Jewish guards who held Jesus in the Jewish court room after the arrest in the garden. Luke writes 'And the men that held Jesus mocked him and beat him'. He tells us what their game was. It was to tie a cloth around his eyes and then clout him, one after another. He was a prophet, let him identify the striker! And then with a delicacy we lack today, Luke draws down the curtain. 'And many other things spoke they against him, reviling him.' Some of us could make guesses, but we refrain.

Then *secondly*, Herod had his fun—Herod the King, Herod the play-boy. Because he could not get a miracle out of Jesus he decided to get something, so with the help of his soldiers he decked him out in comic gorgeous robes and sent him back to Pilate. He would like to see Pilate's face when this comic king re-entered his palace. The thought of it made Herod's day.

Thirdly. No doubt the gorgeous robes put ideas into the heads of Pilate's soldiers. Not for them to mock Jesus as a prophet; they probably could not understand his Aramaic anyway, but a king they knew, and an emperor they knew. So when they cut Jesus down from the whipping post, they propped up the bleeding mass in a corner. A soldier's red cloak, a crown of thorns and a reed for a sceptre completed the picture. The King of the Jews! Then they bowed the knee and did obeisance. Then they spat.

Fourthly, the chief priests, the scribes and the elders mocked him. They had waited till they saw him safely pinned up on the Cross. They were sure then he could not work a miracle. So they started. Matthew tells us this. What they laughed at was Jesus' impotence when nailed to a piece of wood. 'He saved others', they said, 'himself he cannot save.'

Fifthly, the execution squad mocked him; they again would be Romans. They had the last laugh because they had to stand by till the end. Their fun was to offer Jesus drinks, keeping the liquor-soaked sponge just so near and just so far away (you can guess) so as to make a drink impossible. What they too mocked was Jesus' impotence.

There was a day back in Galilee when Jesus was free and the people crowded round admiringly, when he told a story of a man setting out to build a tower. But he miscalculated. He laid the foundation, he set up the walls, but he couldn't finish it; then everybody gathered round to look and laugh; indeed they mocked at him.

That is what was done to Jesus. When the people saw him imprisoned and powerless in the hands of the Rome that broke all opposition with its iron grip, they thought of the promises Jesus had made of the coming of the kingdom of God, and they laughed at him, mocking the apparently ridiculous outcome, a man even without clothes, exhibited on a public gallows for everyone to see.

2. *The Church's mockers*

Today all the fashion is to mock at Christianity. Christianity hasn't stopped war. It hasn't given men bread to eat. It hasn't put a stop to pain. It hasn't stopped untimely deaths. Oh yes, it has some magnificent buildings. Oh yes, it has a magnificent past—but by and large Christianity has duped the masses. 'Pie in the sky when we die.' This will keep the people quiet.

And so the Marxists say, 'Religion is a fine thing—for grandmothers!' And the intellectualists count it puerile. And the sensualists dub it repressive. And the common run of men and women cannot see what it has to do with providing motor cars and money.

So they join hands to mock, each in his own fashion.

Who is right, the mockers or the mocked? Let us look back for a minute at the five groups who mocked at Jesus' impotence—the Jewish court room guards who clouted him, Herod the playboy, Pilate's soldiers after the flogging, the chief priests at the Cross, and the execution squad offering drinks to a dying man who could not reach them. Who is right, the mockers or the mocked?

3. *God's apparent impotence*

But the apparent impotence of Christ *is* a problem. It was not only a problem at Calvary, in another form it is a problem still. Why does not God put a check on the population explosion which must mean more hunger and disease in the end? Why does he allow men to invent and manufacture such diabolical weapons as napalm bombs? Is it that God may be good but that he is actually impotent? Some men think so. Perhaps a great many people think so. That is why they mock. God is asleep. God is dead. God is powerless. Man can sin with impunity. Sin in fact does not exist. 'In the final age there will be men who pour scorn on religion, and follow their own godless lusts.' So the New English Bible in Jude verse eighteen, or in the old words 'They told you there should be mockers in the last time. . . .'

What are we to say about God's apparent impotence? Think of the tower the man in Christ's story began to build and could not finish. Perhaps this is how we ought to view this world. It is an *unfinished* place, and because we do not see yet the other world on the other side of death, what we see on this side appears to be maddeningly futile.

What are we to say about Christ's apparent impotence on the Cross? But was he impotent? Did he not accomplish what no-one else has accomplished? He met the fury of his foes with no kind of hitting back, not even with words. Resistance produces future resistance. But with Jesus the chain reaction was broken. Hate was defeated. So the kingdom of God's love came in at Calvary in the person of its King.

Was Christ therefore impotent after all? Is God impotent after all? Who is right? Who can see through the superficiality to the reality underneath? Is it the mockers, or is it the mocked?

My friends, I know it is easy these days to lose our nerve when so many seem to poke fun at the Church of Christ and make it look ridiculous. Do not fall in with them. One day the Lord of all men will be justified in the sight of all men. For that day let us wait. In this confidence let us stand firm.

LENT

Passion pictures

Every year, round about March we take down from the bookshelves the volume called *Pictures of the Passion* and turn the pages. It is true we have seen them all before many times, but like all masterpieces—and this is what they are—they prove to be inexhaustible. Always they make an impact on the eye, always an impact on the mind, always we find ourselves discovering something fresh.

So we turn the pages. Who is that? *Caiaphas*, of course, representative of established religion, Caiaphas. You can tell him by his clothes. But it is his eyes that hold you. A man's soul shines through his eyes; and these eyes are narrow, gimletty and dark.

We turn the page. And who is that? *Pilate.* No-one could mistake Pilate, clean-shaven—or almost clean, with short cropped hair, jaw set, obviously a Roman. He speaks Latin in a clipped way, and the flood of guttural Hebrew all about him galls him. He loathes all who spout it. Pilate stands for the power of civil Government, but his Procurator's seat isn't safe, and he knows it.

Who comes next? *Herod*, of course, the playboy in the party, propped up on his petty throne by the Imperial Power, but half the time he yawns. It is not much fun being a King, even a puppet King. What he prefers is the easy girls; the kind of man whose eyes undress every woman he meets.

Next, a contrast. *Peter*, Saint Peter, to give him his later title. He is honest as the day, of course, but human; a northerner and a countryman as well. The city types would get him on the run, even a tart could fix him. Poor Peter is at the mercy of all these metropolitan sharks and he knows it. Look at those eyes. Look at those hands.

And then *Barabbas*, a not unfamiliar face today or at any time where agitators are about agitating for people's rights, whether in Bogside, Haarlem, or the Paris suburbs. He mans the barricades, a stop-at-nothing type. When the mob gets worked up, this one comes out on top, the dare-devil sort, the kind of face not open to sweet reason.

The next picture in the album you have to unfold because it is too large to fit into one page, but when you do, it is covered with faces, almost a Michelangelo crowd of faces. And that is what it depicts, *the crowd* taking part in the crucifixion of Jesus, because it did take part. Three out of the five men we have looked at, Caiaphas, Pilate and Barabbas, deliberately used the crowd and were dependent on it.

There is something familiar about this crowd. We are given pictures of crowds almost every day in our newspapers. And nine times out of ten they are protesting, using slogans and captions chalked up on placards carried by the militants. We see this in the passion pictures. And we read the slogans. We can't help reading them. Everyone is meant to read them including Caiaphas and Pilate. Half the captions say 'Crucify Jesus'. The other half say 'Freedom for Barabbas'. We might have known freedom would come in somewhere. It usually does in protests. That is what they are most often about. Freedom for someone to do something, or to be something or to get something. This time it is freedom for Barabbas, the agitator type, and Jesus for the gallows.

1. *The people's assessment*

These passion pictures, of course, are a judgement on the Establishment. My guess is that today every young man would understand that—Caiaphas and Pilate cooking things up to get rid of an awkward intruder who would ask embarrassing questions about truth and sincerity and honesty. But just when everyone is settling down with the villains of the piece all identified, down comes democracy with a disconcerting dénouement. Without that crowd neither Caiaphas nor Pilate would ever have accomplished the crucifixion of Jesus. How many times had they mumbled concerning their intended arrest, 'Not during the Festival, because of the people'? They understood how they needed the people. And they got them, got them where they wanted them. The trials of Jesus took place when their rulers knew the people were asleep. His condemnation took place when the people got swayed with the alternatives of 'Jesus Christ' or 'Jesus Barabbas' placarded before their eyes. And like all crowds that see the issues in simple terms as represented by slogans, as misrepresented by slogans, they opted for the noisy, superficial candidate. They bellowed for the common agitator. The passion story of Jesus is no place from which the people come away with any kind of medals. The people were, in fact, manipulated as a tool, an operation repeated to the present day, sometimes by big business barons.

2. *Peter's assessment*

Where does your pity lie? Where is my pity in all these pictures? Where is your condemnation? Where mine? Is it on

Caiaphas? Is it on Pilate? Is it on Herod? Is it on the crowd? Were they wicked? Were they dupes?

And what about the man whose picture I have left till last? The man up from the country, fair game for all the metropolitan twisters. I refer to Saint Peter. Whom does *he* blame? Where after the crucifixion of the Lord (of whom they cheated him), does he settle the condemnation? And the answer is, he lets them off! No, you can't believe it, but it is true, he lets them off! Listen to him up on his feet in Jerusalem itself addressing a crowd. 'Ye denied the holy and righteous one and asked for a murderer to be granted unto you, and killed the prince of life.' You remember, don't you, the poles, the placards and the protests. But then this—you wait for it—'And now brethren' (brethren! can you believe it!), 'I know that in ignorance you did it as did also your rulers.' (Acts 3.14 ff.)

What has happened? What has happened to Peter, Saint Peter? He has come clean out of the network, the old-boy network in which every man alive is netted, excusing each other, justifying each other, scratching each other's back in turn. Peter sees the situation, not from netted man's disgruntled, offended, self-excusing point of view, but from another standing altogether, the standing ground of God's clean place, the place of his (Peter's) repentance and his (God's) forgiveness.

Peter was no angel in the passion and he knew it. But he did what no others did, no others, that is, in the picture gallery we have been looking at, neither Caiaphas nor Pilate nor Barabbas (as far as we know). Peter acknowledged his guilt and accepted God's forgiveness. It was this that made him the new man, the new strong man, stronger than those metropolitan twisters.

3. *Democracy today*

But what about the crowd? Did they repent? The extraordinary fact is that many of them did. We read that they returned from the crucifixion beating their breasts; on that day, that black day, that bright day, they accepted that democracy is no angel.

Will democracy accept it today? Democracy which is the best form of government we know, will it accept that, nevertheless, it is no angel? Will the people accept that a thing is not necessarily right because it is democratic? It is asking a lot. But the crowd has learnt it before. It learnt at the Cross where many hard lessons are learnt. It could learn it again. And of this we can be absolutely certain. 'If we say that we have no sin, we deceive ourselves, and the truth is not in us: but if we confess our sins, he (God), is faithful and just to forgive us our sins, and to cleanse us from all unrighteousness.'

PALM SUNDAY

The choice

Matthew 21.5 (NEB) '*Here is your king, who comes to you in gentleness, riding on an ass, riding on the foal of a beast of burden.*'

INTRODUCTION

Today our interest is centred upon a procession, a procession in a capital city, a procession on a Sunday and obviously deliberately organized. All this is familiar to any Londoner during the last decade, beginning with the Aldermaston marches. The idea, of course, is to attract attention, attention to people who would not otherwise receive it, people who do not hold the reins of power.

All this is true of a procession we remember on Palm Sunday. But there is one significant difference: no demands are made. If you look at the slow, winding procession that makes its slow, winding way into Jerusalem on Palm Sunday, you will see no placards or poles, no captions, no wage demands; indeed, there are no demands at all. Only an enthusiastic crowd waving palm branches and drawing attention to a person 'riding on the foal of a beast of burden', the equivalent of which today might be a builder's lorry. Here is the king of all those who *do not threaten with demands*, demands for themselves.

And the whole thing, of course, is comic, comic in the popular cynical sense. Ask the Heathrow firemen, ask the railwaymen, ask the schoolteachers. They will stoutly affirm that people only get what they grasp; campaigning, fighting and striking is the only way. And they can show results, wage increases all round. And the rising generation of schoolchildren have had an object lesson set squarely before their eyes. The tough way pays. That is why the procession we remember today will be dubbed by all who understand it as utterly pathetic.

AD 29

1. *Jerusalem's way*

Of course, the ruling clientele in Jerusalem dubbed it as pathetic. You must remember the Jewish nation was up against Rome. It was the underdog, the underprivileged and the subject race of people. And it wanted to be free, free from the hated Roman, free to order its own way of life. And Jerusalem lay there on its rocky eminence outwardly quiescent, but in truth only waiting for the day when it could fly at the cursed Roman and tear his vitals out. Caiaphas was convinced, and all the rulers were convinced that hitting back was the only way for the Jewish nation to realise her national destiny, to strike and strike and strike again.

2. *Christ's way*

Jesus of Nazareth pleaded for another way. That was his significance.

In what is called the annual 'Ethel M. Wood Lecture' in the University of London, Dr G. B. Caird of Mansfield College, Oxford, in 1965 set out convincingly (at least for me) what was the object of Jesus' ministry in Galilee and Judaea. It was to plead with his own nation, the Jewish people, to realise her destiny not by hitting back with weapons, but by making itself a people of justice, mercy and truth, ideals that were enshrined in her scriptural law and prophets.

Palm Sunday then was Jesus' last appeal, his last appeal to the nation, a last appeal in the form of an acted sermon. He was offering himself as King of the peaceful way. That is why he rode a peaceful animal, the foal of an ordinary beast of burden, a domesticated donkey. He was saying in a form that all who have eyes in their heads could see, 'Will you take my way or will you take the way of striking back with weapons?' Such was the choice, the choice of that Palm Sunday. And Jesus knew how Jerusalem would choose. As he thought of it, tears welled up in his eyes as he looked upon that lovely city. Hitting Rome as a policy would mean Rome hitting back. It all happened in AD 70. And as for Jerusalem, the Romans did not 'leave one stone upon another that was not thrown down'. See how Saint Luke puts it.

AD 1970

1. *Striking against human overlords*

As we look out on our nation today, can we be certain that it has chosen the right way in pursuing as it does in many fields the path of wielding the strike weapon? Has the striking by the schoolteachers enhanced the reputation of that calling? Have the sit-downs by the students improved the willingness of public bodies to help where help is needed? Is there a growing sympathy for men in industry who hold the public up to ransom? People only get what they grasp. That is the short view, but the atmosphere can be so poisoned that work in that trade or profession is never quite the same again.

We are not to gather from this that Jesus either let people walk over him or encouraged his disciples to let people walk over them. If you doubt this I would ask you to read what Jesus said to his opponents to their faces. He could tear strips off people. But he did not hold the public to ransom. He certainly did not hold innocent people to ransom, and certainly not little children. Christ *never used other people as a lever to get himself concessions.*

Perhaps there is a time when weapons are necessary. Perhaps

there is a time when to wield the strike weapon is necessary. Certainly I would not say that strikes are always wrong. But I believe that striking as a weapon is far too often used today. We must not forget that striking *is* a weapon, and as such Christ rejected it. And he rejected it because hitting back means hitting back again. This is why our Lord spoke no words of hate upon the Cross to those who hated him. The blows he took to himself and so provoked no like reaction. So peace begins at the Cross, and reconciliation to humanity as well.

All this of course Jerusalem rejected, and it brought no happiness in its wake. This is the message of Palm Sunday, procession Sunday, a message to nations and to groups within those nations. There is always a crowd ready to bellow 'To arms. To arms. Hit back. And hurt.' But thank God there is always the lone man on the donkey, calling for another way. It would have been Jerusalem's wisdom, it would be our wisdom to pay attention to this other way.

2. *Striking against the Lord of heaven*

But I can hear someone saying 'Yes, all very interesting and maybe true, but of what use is it to me? What difference does it make to me? I do not control nations. I do not control groups within nations. What power have I over strikes and protests?'

This I think. Whoever you are, are there not times when you have felt like striking against God, or do I only speak for myself? Life hasn't worked out exactly as we would have wished. There was that opportunity that never came our way. There was that illness just when we were getting going! And scores of 'might have beens'. Do you not know what it means to want to strike against God? Life isn't fair!

There is a case of striking against God in the Bible, a classic case. It is Jonah, called by God to go east to Nineveh, and in protest he goes west; and then in bitter complaint sulks with deep resentment.

There are times when we have felt like that. We even felt

we had a right to strike. But Palm Sunday comes to speak the warning word to us as individuals—do not strike against God. Nothing will come of it. It never has. Christ's way is the acceptance of life as it is, acceptance in faith, faith that God has some purpose or plan in it, difficult though it may be at times to see. But Palm Sunday calls us to peaceful negotiation, yes, even with God. 'Come now, and let us reason together.' It is the way to personal development.

GOOD FRIDAY

God is love

Romans 5.8 '*But God commendeth his love toward us, in that, while we were yet sinners, Christ died for us.*'

Yes, that is the place to *begin* Good Friday, and to *end* Good Friday, in a deep consciousness of the love of God. Of course it is hard unless we take our eyes off the surface of the scene. Outside Jerusalem's wall that day a terrible deed was being perpetrated on a hill shaped like a man's head stripped of all its flesh. What could be more macabre than to drain a man's life out of his body amid that ugliness, close to a garden of graves. Fear, anger, blood-lust, cruelty, callousness, contempt —all the hobgoblins of the nether regions of the human psyche —trooped out that day to spit on Jesus in his dying agony. It is hard, yes frighteningly hard, to see nothing but clouds, darkness and thick clotted beastliness, hard to see the love of God, hard to see any redeeming feature. And it had all happened before. And it has all happened since. Men have been crucified by men in agony, bad men, good men, savages, saints. How in any of these offensive deaths can anyone hope to see the love of God?

1. *The love of God*

Yet that is where we must begin—in the love of God. Otherwise we shall be back with heathen notions of our God, making him a god of terror, a god of pitiless wrath, a god whose untamed nature it is to extract the last drop of pain and punishment from those who rebel against his holy sovereignty. And so come all the dreadful ideas of Christ propitiating an angry God; of God being satisfied with a man's blood as if he were a Shylock; of God and Christ set over against each other, one doing one thing and one another; of God and Christ of different natures, one avenging, the other loving. But across all these *mis*conceptions of Calvary Paul writes one convincing, shattering, initial sentence, 'But God commendeth his love toward us, in that, while we were yet sinners, Christ died for us.' Everything about Good Friday issues from the *love* of God shown in Jesus Christ.

2. *What sin does*

And when was this love demonstrated? When *is* it demonstrated? 'While we were yet sinners.' What does sin mean in practical terms? That is to say, what is the issue of sin? It is separation from God. This is its seriousness. But the Cross shows that *there is nothing that can separate us* from the love of God, not even if we drive sharp iron nails into his hands, bump up the cross with a sickening thud agonising the victim, laugh at him dying in his agony, offer him sour wine he just could not reach. Still he says, 'Father, forgive them, for they know not what they do.' All of which cries aloud across the ages that block us off from Calvary and that Roman gibbet, that no separation from God is too great for God in Christ to reach across. He stretches out his hands of forgiveness to every one; and forgiveness *means* restoring to fellowship, just as sin means breaking it up.

3. *An objective work*

'Christ died for us.' What gallons of ink have been used to discuss in learned treatises *how* we are to interpret the words 'for us'! Did Christ die as our *substitute?* Did he die as our *representative?* Did he die offering the perfect penitence we cannot offer? What is the right answer to these questions?

All are half right and all are half wrong. But the extraordinary fact is that whatever theories are preached, however grossly imperfect, if somehow they convey something of the truth that on his cross Christ did for man what no man can do for himself, that when *he* so died, that death was unique and accomplished an unique result to which the resurrection bore testimony, then new life enters into the human heart, eternal life, life of an eternal quality. Such is the wonder of Good Friday. An unique work was accomplished for man issuing from the love of God. It becomes us all to rest our deepest selves here and in the God made manifest.

EASTER

Two halves

> I Corinthians 15.22 '*As in Adam all die, even so in Christ shall all be made alive.*'

'As in Adam all die. . . .' Well, here is something no-one will argue about! We might not express it in those words, but we know it is true. 'As in Adam all die.'

FIRST HALF

1. *Physical death*

At the present time death holds a strange fascination for a growing number of people. In the last twelve months at least two substantial books have been written about it. Perhaps this is not so strange. Since people have largely abandoned an active belief in God and any life beyond the grave, death appears as its crowning futility. A man, a woman, spends a life-time building up a character, a career and various skills, only to have them swept away by the coronary, the car crash, or worse, the wasting disease. Death crowns the absurdity of human existence.

2. *Moral death*

'As in Adam all die.' I want, however, to go a little further. I want to suggest that not only does this apply to physical existence, but to moral existence as well. 'As in Adam all die.' Of course, the humanist will be up in arms at this. His idea is that man is able, by his own unaided qualities, to lift himself to the highest planes of moral behaviour. According to him, the human stands in no need of the divine. That is why the humanist is called a humanist. He believes in the self-sufficiency of the human. His is the argument for morality *without* religion.

But look around. No doubt the humanist is also looking around. I am sorry for him. Today he must surely be at the point of despair. We have got what he wanted, we have got rid of the old-fashioned trammels of religion; but instead of walking in the uplands of a morally enlightened community, we have instead the permissive society and with it greed, drugs, slovenliness, violence and irresponsibility, which is certainly not what the humanists wanted. They are better men than that! But what they will not face is the truth in my text 'As in Adam all die'. Left to himself alone, man, for all his goodness, nobility and lofty ideals, drifts down to moral death. 'As in Adam all die.' This does not mean there never have been, there are not now, good men without religion. Nor does the drifting down happen overnight, but slowly, little by little, till suddenly people look around them and say 'How on earth has British life come to this sorry state?' The answer is 'Left to itself without God, this is what eventually happens.' 'As in Adam all die.'

SECOND HALF

And somebody wants to say 'But how depressing!' But the text hasn't finished. It goes on 'Even so in Christ shall all be made alive'.

1. *Moral resurrection life*

Now Saint Paul, who wrote these words to the Corinthians

saw this happen in Corinth itself. He saw new life in Christ spring up. Unless you have read about it for yourself, you have no idea what a sink of iniquity Corinth was. We talk about our permissive society but it is nothing in comparison with Corinth, that city of a quarter of a million inhabitants. Ours is a permissive society *frowned on* by religion. Corinth was a permissive society *supported by* religion. If you stood in the market place in Corinth, what impressed you was the mountain 1,900 feet high towering above you, and on its summit, the great Temple of Aphrodite. This was the temple of the religion of sex. One thousand girls were kept there dedicated to the goddess, and their processions, rituals and solicitudes so aroused the male public that the phrase 'to live like a Corinthian' meant to be a habitual fornicator. It was in this kitchen-sink community that Paul saw men and women turn to live like Christ. And not only in Corinth but in Ephesus and Philippi and Thessalonica and Rome. 'As in Adam all die', that is true, but so is this true, 'even so in Christ shall all . . .' yes, people of all kinds, 'even so in Christ shall all be made alive'.

2. *Physical resurrection life*

Now if the *first* part of the text 'As in Adam all die' refers both to the physical and the moral, why should not the *second* part also refer to the moral and the physical? 'Even so in Christ shall all be made alive.' I have referred to moral resurrection in Corinth and other cities (a miracle if ever there was one). I refer now to the physical.

The meaning here is that death is not the end. When we come up to the gate, as we all shall, we shall find that it *is* a gate and not a blank wall. Death is not journey's end, it is a frontier post. It marks the cross-over from two halves of existence and what lies on the other side is the part we do not now see. These bodies we shall not take with us. Nor will they somehow be resuscitated on the other side. They remain here because they belong to the stuff of a material world. But the person, the individual, whatever it is that makes you you and me me, is raised and clothed with a body adequate for the conditions of its new existence. 'As in Adam all die, even so in Christ shall all be made alive.'

The key words are 'in Christ'. This is what happens 'in Christ'. Christ was a man and Christ died. *But Christ also rose again.* So we also shall. . . . Ah! but you can't prove it, Mr Preacher, you can't prove it! No, I can't—but it looks like it, doesn't it? It looks uncommonly like it. After all, if Christ did *not* rise again on Easter Day, how on earth can you explain the rise of the Christian Church? How on earth can you explain its growth in Corinth? So I take the jump with the Church. I take the jump into the faith, the 'Easter faith'. 'As in Adam all die, even so in Christ shall all be made alive.'

APPLICATION

And this is the remarkable result. When we do take this leap of faith, life comes together, holds together, and begins to make sense. Therefore, as an adult I hold to this faith myself, and I invite you to do the same. I invite you to retighten the structures of your faith. There are forces in plenty ready to knock it down. Do not let that happen. We need the faith. Individuals need it. Society needs it. Britain needs it. 'As in Adam all die, even so in Christ shall all be made alive.'

EASTER

The laughing angel

> Matthew 28.2 '*And behold, there was a great earthquake: for the angel of the Lord descended from heaven, and came and rolled back the stone from the door, and sat upon it.*'

I wonder how many of us have in our memories an object which sums up for us a whole scene from the past. It could be a special kind of armchair in which one of our parents used to sit, and whenever we see that kind of chair our minds go back to the old home. Somehow, that chair, or that kind of chair, symbolizes to us home, parents and childhood. And if the truth were told, we aren't quite sure whether we like it or not. Somehow it has a poignancy.

Studdart Kennedy, the famous chaplain of World War I, tells of the uncomfortable feeling the red light on the back of a train always gave him. This was because he used to work through those terrible troop trains standing in the sidings at Rouen ready to be taken up to the front lines. They were jammed with soldiers, mostly young boys only eighteen or twenty years old, half of them afraid, all of them whistling to keep their courage up. And beginning at the front coach he would work right through every compartment with two haversacks, one on each shoulder, the one containing New Testaments which he gave away, and the other packets of Woodbines, that is, cigarettes, which he also gave away; which is why they nicknamed him 'Woodbine Willie'. When he left the last compartment, climbed down on to the track, his haversacks empty, he looked back at the rear of the last coach on which was the red light. The red light. Then slowly the train would pull out and that red light appeared smaller and smaller. The last he saw of that train was the red light. It symbolized for him a train load of men being hauled to the slaughter with their New Testaments and Woodbines. And of course many of them, sometimes almost all of them, did not return. For Studdart Kennedy, a red light symbolized Rouen and troop trains.

The women and the Apostles who loved Jesus of Nazareth had a symbol in *their* experience which similarly summed up for them everything about that terrible crucifixion on Skull Hill outside the city wall of Jerusalem. It wasn't an armchair, it wasn't a red light; it was for them a stone, a large, thick, circular stone, in fact they were particularly impressed by its size. Not even three or four young women together could move a stone of this size. And even men would need the instrument stone-masons use. This was the stone rolled in the groove before the carved-out tomb in which the body of Jesus was laid after his crucifixion and removal from the cross. Everything they felt about Good Friday was epitomized in that stone.

1. *The message of the stone*

What did it say? I mean, what did the stone say?

It said, it does not matter how strong a man is, and Jesus was strong. It does not matter how good a man is, and Jesus was good, nor how kind, law-abiding and constructive, everything, the good and the bad alike, comes in the end to a little hole in the ground, six feet of earth by two feet, the Crematorium to the north of London or the south of London. The end of all royalty, nobility *or* decadence is a graveyard and a stone rolled upon the top of it.

What did the stone say as they looked at it rolled into place on Friday night in its well-cut groove? It said, there is nothing other than the power of men. Men cut out that grave, men took down that body, men wound it round and buried it, men rolled the stone into its place. Yes, and the authorities in Jerusalem came and sealed that stone with their official seal, and set a guard to keep intruders out. No-one would come and steal that body and talk of resurrections, miracles or a world of spirit. All power ends with the death of man. Nothing else exists. And even Jesus was barred away for ever, trapped behind a stone. The stone marked the point where all power peters out for ever.

2. *The message of the angel*

But what does Easter Day come round to tell us? Many things. But first, that the stone was rolled away. It was the first thing that the women noticed when they reached the grave at daybreak, just as it was the last thing they had noticed when they left the tomb on Friday night.

The stone was rolled away.

Which means, of course, that all the stone epitomized was rolled away—death as the end, a hole in the ground as the end, human power as all the power there is in life. The rolling away of the stone proclaims that there is a completely different dimension in the universe which makes for entirely different possibilities. And so St Matthew's Gospel piles the imagery on, making the stone a symbol. All right, you will have other symbols to stress the other dimension breaking in. How else can you stress it but with symbols? 'And behold, there was a great earthquake: for the angel of the Lord descended from heaven, and came and rolled back the stone from the door, and sat upon it.'

I don't know if angels laugh, and it would be a silly question because angels are symbols, but if they do, that angel sitting on that stone outside the grave of Jesus was sitting laughing—you think a stone is the end, you think you know all the answers about human existence. You think you have solved all the riddles by speaking no more of heaven 'up there' and earth 'down here'. All right, look back at the stone. It is rolled away—'Behold, there was a great earthquake: for the angel of the Lord descended from heaven, and came and rolled back the stone from the door, and sat upon it.' This scripture rubs our noses in our own sophistication.

3. *The message of Easter*

My friends, on this Easter Day let me remind you that all the limits we set to the span of man's life and scope of power in this world are misconceived. There is a life out there which is also with us now, life of a different quality, life of strange, surpassing power and, most surprising of all, a power available to people now. Matter, food and money are not the final word. The stone which says they are was rolled away on the first Easter Day, and a smiling angel sat on the top of it.

I find as I go about London and read the newspapers and watch the television and sometimes go to the theatre, I find that an enormous cloud of depression has settled on people's hearts and I think I understand the reasons. I, too, could be downcast when I think of what our nation has become. There is little greatness in it now.

But we are reckoning without God. We are reckoning men and money and machines have the final word. But they haven't. The resources of all inspiration, inventiveness and nobility is with us still, the spirit of God alive, gloriously alive, eternal and powerful. We need not and must not give up hope. Human considerations, failures and limitations are not the end. There can be an earthquake, the break-up of existing patterns, stones can be rolled away and an angel sit on top of every one of them, as if to say, 'I told you so!'

EASTER

Two ways of seeing

> John 16.16 (NEB) *'A little while, and you see me no more; again a little while, and you will see me.'*

Here at least is a situation in which many of us will be ready to join the disciples of Jesus. When he uttered the words I have quoted they 'said one to another, "What does he mean by this: 'A little while, and you will not see me, and again a little while, and you will see me,' and by this: 'Because I am going to my Father'?" So they asked, "What is this 'little while' that he speaks of? We do not know what he means." '

Looking back, the words, however, do not seem all that difficult to us because we have the advantage of hindsight. We can understand how Jesus left his disciples for a 'little while' through the gate of death, and then came back for 'a little while' after his resurrection, to be seen by them during what are called 'the forty days'. This is the Christian tradition.

1. *Two kinds of eyes*

There is, however, a deeper level at which these words are to be understood. They are set in a context about the Holy

Spirit, and what they refer to is two ways of looking at Jesus, firstly with the eyes of the body, secondly with the eye of the spirit. There are, in fact, two quite distinct Greek words used here for 'seeing', the first word referring to the natural eye, and the second to the spiritual eye. So the text could read 'A little while, and you will not see me with the natural eye; again a little while and you will see me with the spiritual eye.'

These are not two diametrically opposed ways of seeing Jesus, and it may be that most people like the Apostles who come fully to see Jesus do so by passing from the one to the other. What, however, is important is that we cannot stop simply seeing Jesus with the eye of the body if we are to appreciate him, we must see him with the eye of the spirit.

Let me spell this out a little more clearly.

2. *The natural eye*

First, seeing Jesus with the eye of the body, the natural eye. Notice how I speak about *Jesus* in this connection, using his common earthly name with no titles attached. I do so because I am referring to the man who walked about in Galilee and Judaea in the first thirty years of our era, eating, sleeping and mixing with people as other men do. In other words, I am referring to the historical man, the Jesus of history (to use a loaded phrase). This is what his contemporaries saw with their physical, natural eyes.

We in our day cannot exactly do that. Jesus does not belong to our contemporary scene. But we try very hard, and some scholars have given almost their whole lives to the attempt to represent for modern man the historical Jesus, how he spoke, what he taught, what clothes he wore, the life situation in which he worked. Dr Albert Schweitzer wrote a famous book called *The Quest of the Historical Jesus*, summing up an enormous attempt throughout the nineteenth century in Europe to try and see again, as it were, what Jesus was really like. And this fascinates even to our own day. You remember the popularity of Pasolini's film *The Gospel according to Saint Matthew*.

Now it is true, of course, that a few followers of Jesus in his lifetime on earth did see through to his significance. Peter, in particular, called out at Caesarea Philippi his confession 'Thou art the Christ'. For the most part, however, people only saw Jesus in the days of his flesh with the natural eye, what I have called the first way of seeing him.

3. *The spiritual eye*

There came however, *the second way of seeing him*, seeing him with the eyes of the Spirit. This occurred after his death, resurrection and ascension. When those events took place they saw him not simply as an extraordinary man, but as the Christ and the Messiah, and they called him 'Lord', a title that only occurs rarely in the pre-resurrection narratives. In other words, they saw the *significance* of Jesus, they saw what he meant for them, and the indication of what they saw is marked by the titles they gave him, 'Christ', or 'Jesus Christ', or 'the Lord Jesus Christ', or even 'My Lord and my God'.

There are two ways then of seeing Jesus—with the natural eye and with the spiritual eye, neither being naturally exclusive; but this is the point. If we have not seen him in the second way, if we have not seen him with the eye of the spirit, we have scarcely seen his significance at all.

4. *How to see with the spiritual eye*

And someone says 'Yes, this is all very interesting in an academic kind of way. And I am glad, too, that we do not all have to become historical research students to appreciate this great central figure of the Christian faith, but tell me, how do I start seeing him with the spiritual eye?' How does an ordinary man or woman begin?

The answer is *by commitment of life to him*. In a very real way Christ is incognito. He is part hidden. He does not lie on the surface. You can't go along and discover him as you might find a coin on the pavement outside. That is why the people of his day in Galilee and Judaea failed to recognize him. They passed him by and some crucified him. Christ is partly incognito. He may be seen with the natural eye and *not* be seen with the spiritual eye at the same time. But this is the point, he discloses himself to those who commit themselves to him in personal trust and obedience.

How do I know Jesus is the Christ? By going out and doing what he told us to do. *Doing*, that is the key. *Doing* love to my neighbour, *doing the work* of each day in the confidence that all is in God's hands, doing justly in the common affairs of life; this is committing myself in obedience to the Christian way, and in so doing I see Jesus, not merely as a wonderful man who lived long ago, but as Christ the Saviour now.

EASTER

Jesus or Christ?

This evening we think of *another evening* because it has never been forgotten. In fact this is why we think of it again, so that *we* shall not forget it, because it has something important to say, especially in the modern climate of opinion.

INTRODUCTION

Ten men that evening were together in an upper room, ten Apostles. It was probably the same room where the Holy Communion was instituted, and certainly they were the same men; but two were missing on this occasion, Judas, who was dead by now, and Thomas who was depressed. Unexpectedly in that company the risen Christ appeared. They saw him, they could touch him, they could put fingers into the wound marks in his hands and feet. Clearly it was no disembodied spirit they experienced.

But Thomas couldn't believe it when they told him, and they told him out of pity because they couldn't bear to see one of the company so terribly downcast. Thomas, however, went so far as to assert the only conditions on which he would believe in the resurrection. 'Unless I see the mark of the nails in his hands, unless I put my finger into the place where the nails were, and my hand into his side, I will not believe it.'

1. *The real problem*

Our first reaction to this may be to write Thomas off as one of those naïve people who assert that they will only believe in what they can see. 'Seeing is believing.' And the notion is so patently absurd that it scarcely seems worth repeating, were it not true that people do exist who make such assertions. They only need to be asked if they have any brains, because they certainly can't see them! And if there is outer space, because it certainly is not visible!

We do Thomas a grave injustice if we count him as that kind of fool. It is far more likely that Thomas really did believe that Mary Magdalene had seen something in the garden on Easter morning. It is far more likely that he accepted that the two disciples on the Emmaus road *had* been joined by some spiritual being. And the ten Apostles in the upper room really were made aware of a divine presence in their midst. Thomas was a believer in God, in the spirit world, in angels as real heavenly beings. After all, there was evidence in plenty for all this in the Old Testament.

This is what Thomas could not accept—that the Being experienced by various groups and individuals on Easter Day was *the same being* as was crucified, that is, Jesus of Nazareth, the Jesus he knew, the historical man.

2. *The wrong solution*

And doubt has frequently squeezed its way through by making a gap between these two figures, the spiritual Christ and the historical Jesus. The argument runs like this: There was a man called Jesus of Nazareth, the world's greatest teacher, saint and martyr. There is also, always has been, always will be, the mystical Christ, that is to say the divine spirit, pervading all life, time and space. The life of Jesus of Nazareth was simply the point at which this eternal Christ was most vividly encountered. But they are not one and the same; Jesus lived, died and was buried, like all men, but the eternal Christ, the eternal divinity, the eternal spirit is from everlasting to everlasting.

This was the view of Jesus and of Christ that had squeezed through into the mind of Thomas the Apostle and was making him miserable. And it is not difficult to see why it gave him no joy; there was no resurrection in it, nothing new in it, everything was left as it was before, a man had come and gone in whose life the eternal spirit could be encountered. Men like that had been met since the dawn of history. There was nothing new.

And Thomas' interpretation of the events of Easter Day has been followed all down the ages by subtle minds who hereby found a way of not believing in the resurrection of Jesus. Greek philosophy with its notions that matter is inherently evil came in to support it. It asked, how could Jesus with a material body of flesh and blood be divine? Only a body-less spirit can be that! And so strong a hold did this view take, even a hundred years after the first Easter, that the fourth Gospel was largely written to combat it.

3. *The right solution*

But how does it all end—in the Gospel narrative I mean? By the Christ appearing once more in the same upper room, this time with Thomas present. And Thomas looked at Christ —and Christ looked at Thomas. Now what is the answer? Who was it before Thomas' eyes? Jesus of Nazareth, or an appearance of the eternal mystical Christ? Thomas looked at the wound marks. Then he heard the Christ address him. 'Thomas, reach your finger here: see my hands; reach your hand here and put it into my side; be unbelieving no longer, but believe.'

That did it! Thomas cried out 'My Lord and my God!' He knew then that Jesus of Nazareth and the eternal Christ are one and the same being. Jesus *is* the Christ. The resurrection had taken place. Something utterly and absolutely new had occurred on this plane of history, giving a clue to the mystery of life.

CONCLUSION

And someone wants to say 'What a fuss about nothing! I always have believed that Jesus and Christ are one and the same person. After all, we speak of Jesus Christ.' Good! Then you believe in the resurrection because this is what the two names together imply.

But some people *want to deny* the Easter faith. They do not want to believe in a resurrection. They won't have anything to do with miracles. Yet they can't deny that Jesus of Nazareth actually existed, or that he was a great moral teacher, a saint and a martyr. So what do they do? They squeeze through between Jesus the man and Christ the eternal spirit by an intellectual feat and think to bring themselves satisfaction. But does it? Does it bring satisfaction and joy and vitality? Look back at Thomas; he tried that way and he failed. Christian joy only comes through believing in the resurrection of Jesus who is the Christ. That is what the story this evening comes to tell us. The resurrection of Jesus is essential to our Christian faith. We must believe it.

EASTER

The Christ of experience

2 Corinthians 5.16 '*Though we have known Christ after the flesh, yet now henceforth know we him no more.*'

INTRODUCTION

In the last few years there has been a tendency for the number of communicants at Christmas to be growing, and for the number at Easter to be declining.

Why is this? Is it because of the Christmas tree, the carols, the lovely idea of a baby in a manger? Is it sentiment that brings more people at Christmas? Is it that the spring weather at Easter is more favourable to outdoor activities? Or is it, as I fear it may be, that we really do not understand how and why it is that no season compares at all in depth of meaning and importance for us with what happened on the first Good Friday and Easter Day?

What did happen? A superficial judgement could be that on Easter Day a *happy ending* was provided to an otherwise tragic story. Everything turned out all right in the end. Upon which I am bound to say, if that is all it means, I do not wonder that people with an experience of how grey life can be turn away disappointed; life is not like that.

Or we could assume that what Easter Day supremely teaches is that there is *a life to come* beyond this life. And that is true, gloriously true. But people believed in immortality of a kind long before Jesus walked this earth. The Pharisees believed it in Jesus' day.

No, what Easter provides is a *complete transformation* of the way we look at Christian discipleship. This is what St Paul meant when he wrote to the Corinthians, 'Though we have known Christ after the flesh, yet now henceforth know we him no more.' Let us think about this.

a THREE NEGATIVE INTERPRETATIONS OF EASTER

1. First, Easter implies that the Christian Church is not primarily *a historical or an antiquarian society*. That is to say, our first concern is not to find out all the details we can about Jesus of Nazareth. His earthly life is past. It actually took place nearly two thousand years ago. We cannot know about him in any other way than we can know of other historical figures, Caesar Augustus, Charlmagne, Galileo. And if we could put ourselves in complete touch with Jesus we should be dismayed. For one thing, we should not understand the language he spoke. We should not find ourselves in harmony with the social customs and manners he observed. We should be bewildered by his ignorance of things we take for granted, like the telephone, electric light and broadcasting.

Looking round Penshurst Place a short time ago and being struck by a painting there of Queen Elizabeth I, I wondered what we should make of her, or she of us, *if* we actually met in the flesh? Four hundred years is a long time. But Jesus lived two thousand years ago and in a different country. I am glad, therefore, to be able to tell you that Christianity is not historical research into an historical figure, though that has its part to play. 'Though we have known Christ after the flesh, yet now henceforth know we him no more.'

2. Nor does Christianity mean *trying to copy* Jesus of Nazareth.

I shall never forget my first visit to the Chelsea Flower Show, now many years ago. To me it was one of the most absurd experiences I have had. As I passed from tent to tent and saw the floral exhibits on display I nearly collapsed with laughter. I had been accustomed to quite attractive flowers all my life. I had even grown a few and been quite pleased with the results. But here at Chelsea at bench after bench my eyes dwelt on the most fantastic specimens. They were huge, they were perfect, they were dazzling. And when I thought of my own efforts they seemed ludicrous, if not pathetic, and my reaction was to give up gardening altogether. The perfection at Chelsea crushed me.

To look at the life of Jesus could have that effect—I mean to look at him and be told that is what you must be like if you are to bear the name of Christian. Our reply could only be a deep sigh, or even a derisive smile. 'Sorry, but it is all miles away from anything I can ever achieve.'

3. Nor in the third place is Christianity *obedience to specific rules* of behaviour which Jesus devised. He did not leave us such a blue-print. How could he? The world in which he lived knew nothing of joint stock banking, nothing of nationalization, nothing of our slaughter on the roads, nothing of atomic warfare, nothing of space travel, every one of them matters which these days occupy the forefront of our minds. Jesus could not lay down rules for a way of life of which he knew nothing. Whatever he left us in his teaching (and it is

certainly so profound that scholars are still weighing its wisdom), it was not a book of rules of conduct, and Christianity cannot be described in these terms.

b. A POSITIVE INTERPRETATION OF EASTER

This then is the truth. It is not a man in the historical past whom we try to discover, emulate and copy—this is not the essence of Christianity. 'Though we have known Christ after the flesh, yet now henceforth know we him no more.' Why not? The answer is because Easter has taken place and we have instead of the Jesus of history, the living and eternal Christ.

I am not saying Jesus of Nazareth is unimportant. I am not saying that what he did and what he said two thousand years ago is of little consequence nowadays. I am not saying Jesus and Christ are two different people. And if there are any theologians here, I am not opposing the Christ of theology to the Jesus of history—the fashion of nineteenth-century Liberalism.

1. *The risen Christ of experience*

What I am saying is that we do not have to delve into the past to find God. He is here with us. Christ is risen. And where we find him is in current experience: in that moment when we thought the bottom had fallen out of life and we discovered it hadn't; in that time when we felt strangely guided to pursue a certain path and, contrary to all expectation, it turned out to be the right one for us; in that unbelievable strength which we drew upon from our inner being when our backs were up against the wall; in that astonishing sense of forgiveness which cancelled out the weight of guilt concerning some past deeds, through the hearing of the Gospel. These things are true. They happen. They happen to people we know. This is where I feel at one with that modern controversial figure Rudolph Bultmann. If you want a technical word it is existential religion. It is what I have preached for years from this pulpit.

2. *An appeal for openness to God*

So here is the message. We do not have to delve into the past to find God. God was revealed in Jesus to show what God is like now—God, who is the source of all our life and is everywhere round about us, closer than our hands and feet. The right course is to be open to him. It is possible to be shut to him. Resentment is a shutter, unbelief is a shutter, flippancy is a shutter. But if we are open to God who cares for us and will not lose us, we shall be found by him and live for him and rejoice in him. This is the Easter message, a contemporary, relevant, energising thing, something which makes us new men, or as Paul put it—

SUMMARY

'Yea, though we have known Christ after the flesh, yet now henceforth know we him no more. *Therefore* if any man be in Christ, he is a new creature: old things are passed away; behold, all things are become new.'

EASTER

Bereavement is a storm

1. *Storms*

For my first eighteen years I lived within the sound of the North Sea. Now I am a Londoner, yet the sea still holds me in a grip of love and dread. I remember its moods: the green smoothness of a summer evening, the grey anger of a winter storm. I have watched a ship break up in the waves. I have lain awake at night haunted by a ship's distress rockets on the Scroby sands. I recall what my grandfather told me, how at Dunwich when he was a boy, on a stormy night, they said you could hear the bells of the many churches under the sea off that point on the Suffolk coast.

A storm is a terrifying experience. No wonder the coastguard hoists a black cone to signal it. Bereavement is a storm. It can be more frightening than dying, more alarming than death. We may even face the latter with equanimity. And not the least part of the terror of bereavement is that like a storm it blows up suddenly. There is the sudden grinding of brakes, the splintering of glass, the crushed-in bonnet—but worse, far worse, not all the occupants of those two cars in the head-on collision will survive. This is the sudden price too often demanded by mobility in our modern world.

2. *Action required*

What can we do about it? Perhaps three things. *First*, preparation. He is a foolish man who thinks no storms will come. And when they do, to turn then to the coastal engineers is useless. The concrete walls with their piers must be set up on the calm days, the breakwaters bolted into position before the sea runs high. So too, we must build up our religious faith when all our friends and families are happily around us. We must wrestle *then* with the hope and promise of life beyond the grave, and come to firm faith conclusions.

Secondly, we must exercise courage when the storm breaks. Others have faced storms before. Others have come through before. It is never any use running before the storm in the open sea, the ship must head into the waves or cast out an anchor and ride it out. Manly courage, womanly courage is required in bereavement. And do not confuse dryness of the eye for lack of feeling. Some of the most shallow weep most. The dry-eyed may be the most courageous.

Thirdly, patience. It is the nature of storms to blow themselves out. Of course they leave marks behind them. There may be a trail of debris along the water's edge. Constable was never quite the same after his wife died. His later pictures of Salisbury Cathedral lack the fresh greens of his earlier paintings. But a calm always follows. And we should wait for it in bereavement before making changes or decisions in our own environment. Always wait till the wind abates.

3. *The protecting faith*

The most important requirement is to build up and keep in repair our Easter faith. Christ died and he rose again. To hold to this makes the fundamental difference in bereavement. But do not imagine it will *remove* the storm. Do not think it will take away our human sorrow. Remember Jesus wept at the graveside of Lazarus his friend. What the breakwater does is break up the *violence* of the floodwater and so protect the coastline. This is what faith does, exercised with courage and patience. It protects us from the most dangerous inroads of personal loss and helps us to bring our ship, weather-beaten no doubt, limping maybe, into calmer and more navigable waters after the storm, where useful service still remains.

WHITSUNDAY

Catching the wind

John 3.8 (NEB) '*The wind blows where it wills.*'

This is true, isn't it? The wind blows where it wills. I mean H.M. Government is unable to arrange that for the next four weeks we shall enjoy gentle zephyrs from the south, and after that gentle north-easters to keep us cool in July. And neither the scientists nor the meteorologists can change the direction or the strength of the wind. And computors won't help. 'The wind blows where it wills.'

Jesus said the action of God in the world is like that. 'The wind blows where it wills.' What is more, he implied that a proper word for the description of God is 'pneuma' which means wind or breath or spirit. That is how we experience God. We experience him as wind. Something you can't control or organize.

But suppose God *is* like that! Suppose God acts like the wind! Suppose the writer of the fourth Gospel was correct in his interpretation of the experience of Christ and of religious experience in general. It happens in the way it will and not according to any preconceived plan. Suppose this is correct! What then?

1. *Free religion and organized religion*

That is the question the third chapter of St John's Gospel poses, in a story which looks simple but is really profound. Two men confront each other after dark, perhaps on a roof-top, perhaps with the wind refreshing their faces when the city heat of the day had died down—Jesus and Nicodemus in Jerusalem.

And remember that of these two, Jesus was the *free* man, the man from up-country, the man from the hills, the man from the desert experience; wrestling with God and purpose and faith out under the stars, kneeling down on the rocks or the heather, the wind blowing in his face. And Nicodemus was the ecclesiastical man, the man from the Temple, the man from the theological library, the man accustomed to proper forms and ceremonies proper to the ecclesiastical season. Two figures stand on the roof-top, one representing the free action of God's spirit, 'the wind blows where it wills', the other representing organized religion, its authority and its order.

2. *The choice between the two*

And the tendency of modern man is to want the easy choice. Almost all the sympathy for organized religion has run out. Nicodemus gets scarcely any following for what he has to offer. If we are to have religion (and not everyone is sure about that), it must be a purely private affair, bubbling up or bubbling down as it thinks fit, with no creed, culture or theology to inform it. Today the cry could almost be reduced to a slogan—'Religion if you must, yes, but only if unorganized.'

And you look at Nicodemus, the ecclesiastical man, the Establishment man, the man with a long tradition of culture and learning behind him, marked out in the cut of his clothes, the manner of his speaking, even the appearance of the lines on his face. Has he not something of value which he stands for? After all, if you break up all organized religion will you not lose what religion you have? If you give way to individualism how will you preserve contact with the history from which our faith is sprung and without which we should have no faith at all? Water is certainly necessary for life and not a bucket (you can live without buckets), but you need a bucket in which to carry the water. Nicodemus, you have something on your side!

The religion of the Spirit! And the religion of the organized Church! These are the two sides Whitsunday brings to our attention. And not only in the Nicodemus story, but on Whitsunday itself, the birthday of the organized Church *and* the birthday of the coming of the Spirit. What will you decide? To which aspect will you pin your hopes?

3. *The resolution of conflicting approaches*

I have not the slightest hesitation in saying that if we look only to organized religion, by which I mean religion as a structure of organizing goodness, we shall be doomed to disappointment. That, I think, is why Jesus said to Nicodemus, the ecclesiastical man, 'You must be born again'.

On the other hand, if we imagine this means that all organization in religion must be broken up or allowed to decay, our churches and cathedrals becoming museums, I think we are wrong. All life, and this includes spiritual life, must be organized if it is to survive. You cannot go on if you do not organize for tomorrow's needs.

This surely is the way—to grasp firmly the principle that the purpose of all organized religion is not itself, it does not exist to perpetuate itself, *but to catch the wind of God's Spirit blowing* where it will.

Think of the situation like this. Think of London's churches not as bits of self-propelled machinery, but as sails of windmills of different kinds and different shapes set up all over London catching the wind, without which no turning of the machinery inside the mills can take place.

Is the aim of the organization of this place to catch the wind of the Spirit, or is it only to perpetuate ecclesiastical machinery? Upon the answer to this question depends whether or not the Churches will be effective in the nineteen-seventies.

We cannot produce the wind which is God's Spirit, we can only organize to catch it blowing where it wills.

WHITSUNTIDE

The Church of the future

> Zechariah 2.1 '*And I lifted up mine eyes and saw, and behold a man with a measuring line in his hand.*'

I have seen that man quite a number of times, that is to say, I have had experiences of him myself, and I have read about him in history books. He appears in every historical period, and it is important to recognize him. I will tell you who he is. He is the man who knows exactly where the boundaries of the Church are to run, and the limits of doctrine to stand. He is the man who plans for the future with the measurements of the past. And you think he must be an old man, but surprisingly enough, in this vision of Zechariah, he is a young man; which is a reminder that it is not simply age which colours a man's mind, but a man's mind which colours his vision.

1. *The vision of Zechariah*

Let us spell this out a little more clearly. The Jewish nation had been languishing in the mud flats of Mesopotamia where they had been deported as a result of military defeat. Their national life had been broken up, their Temple destroyed and their hope of the future had become nothing but an ash heap. But the Jewish nation received there the second surprise of their history. The edict which bound them in exile was cancelled, and they returned home to rebuild the life that lay in ruins.

But how? They thought they knew how. And all the efforts Zechariah saw seemed to him to embody themselves in the vision of one young man with a measuring line in his hand, measuring out where the limits of the new Jerusalem would be, where the walls would arise and where work would begin, the place, in fact, where the boundaries had stood in the past.

Then two angels appeared, and one called to the other and said 'Run, speak to this young man, saying "Jerusalem shall be inhabited as villages without walls by reason of the multitude of men and cattle therein."' In other words, stop your measuring. It is all waste of time. The walls will not simply stand where they were before, indeed, you are not to think in terms of walls at all. In the new Jerusalem, in the city of our dreams, the cohesive force will not be an exterior wall but God at the centre, himself holding men together by his own attraction, and this will make the walls of fire round about.

2. *A constricting power*

There have always been people ready to pronounce just where the boundary wall of the Church is to run. It ran here in the past, so it must run here in the future, and outside that wall no salvation, no safety! This has been the main tendency of Catholicism.

There have always been those who are quite sure how doctrines must be formulated. This must be believed, that must be subscribed to, just as it has always been for four hundred years. This has been the tendency of Protestantism.

And there are individuals who are quite sure that God can and will only be real to them in certain clearly marked ways which they have experienced before and only through spiritual leaders who belong to their camp and use their expressions.

All these groups of people, Catholic, Protestant, Pietists, are replicas of the man with the measuring line marking out just where the limits of God's actions are to be, in fact, just where those limits have always been. And the messenger of God (because that is what an angel is) runs up to each, begging him to drop the measuring line. We don't know where the limits of God's action will be, it is not for us to mark off the boundaries of the future by keeping our eyes on the boundaries of the past.

3. *A cohesive power*

And more important still—to protect God's work there should not be a constrictive power on the circumference, keeping men in, but a cohesive force at the centre holding men together. That cohesive force we know as the spirit of Jesus Christ. He draws men, he holds men. He draws them in different ways, he holds them in different ways. He draws all sorts of men, and we have no idea what are the limits of his influence, and therefore of his saving power, so we had better not try to draw them with any kind of measuring line. There is only one fact to hold on to, the fact of Christ. It is *this centre* we must establish. The outside walls can look after themselves. Our need is to be sure of Christ. Then this vision of Zechariah will come true. The future for the Church will be much greater than we with our measuring lines could ever possibly imagine. The important necessity is to make Christ central and to trust his spirit, after which no limits can ever be determined.

TRINITY

Worship

Isaiah 40.25 '*To whom then will you liken me?*'

INTRODUCTION

Some time ago we were given on television a photographic account of a revisit to the Bridge over the River Kwai, that terrible place in the last war where so many British and allied prisoners poured out their lives building a railway for Japanese war supplies. That bridge remains as one of the horror spots of the world. Now the railway is used to convey market produce down to the coast, and trade is flourishing. But the shot in the film which stuck in my mind was the picture of the railway's end. I ought not to have been surprised, of course. That railway had to end as all railways end in a pair of buffer stops, a stout plank of wood and a pile of stone chippings. But it all seemed so dull, so flat, so ordinary after the terrible drama of the bridge, the prisoners, the deaths, the disease, the meanness and the heroism all mixed up together in an atmosphere of dysentery and cruelty. And this was the end of all that 'blood, sweat, toil and tears', a pair of buffer stops, a stout plank of wood and a pile of loose stone chippings.

1. *No dead-end with God*

It is possible to see life in those terms, a heroic struggle, a long drawn-out alternation of sunshine and cloud, of happiness and pain, a record of achievement in business and family; but it all runs down to nothing, a mere dead end, a pair of buffer-stops, a plank of wood and a pile of loose stone chippings.

But this Sunday says something entirely different. It says there is no end, no dead end, no final stop. And this because God is in our midst and God is limitless. 'To whom then will you liken me, whom set up as my equal, says the Holy One.? So wrote Isaiah. God cannot be delineated, made analagous to anything or copied. God is the eternal, unfathomable, immeasurable, inexplicable one. Without God there must be a ceiling, a buffer stop and a final rung, but not when God is in the world. With him there is no searching of his way, no plumbing of his depth, no measuring of his height. That is why without God the world comes to a dead end, but with God it has infinite possibilities.

Now all the tendency in our day is to banish God, or at least the notion of God. The latter, of course, is all we can do, but the outcome is not liberation. It is flatness, 'dead-endness' and limitation. And this is cramping and crushing. Such was the experience of the Jewish exiles on the mud flats of the river

Chebar where they were imprisoned. And to meet this condition the prophet spoke of God, not the god in our pockets, not a god we can make an image of (the prophet spent no little time lampooning that whole idea), but the great God we cannot tape at all. With the unfathomable God in our midst, there is no dead end.

2. *Places of worship*

What this means is that for the health of society *places of worship* are needed, places where we can come and sit and kneel and stand and stay quiet and listen and think; but above all peer through into something beyond our finitude. We need places of worship. We need places of which we can say 'Yes, that is *my* place of worship.'

Of course it is a good idea to visit other churches sometimes, to see other buildings, to hear other preachers and listen to different kinds of music. Everybody is better for a holiday and a change from routine. But when you visit you are looking around, judging and estimating—you have to do this—but when you are in your own place of worship, because it is familiar, your mind, your heart, your soul can move away, clean away to God, the eternal one. So you are lifted out of your finitude, your staleness and your 'dead-endness'.

3. *The purpose of liturgy*

And this is *the purpose of liturgy* with its regular repetition. You get used to it. You half know the words. They are partly inside you. And so you can let go of them and drift out and away and up in mind to God and his indescribable majesty. This is worship. It does something to you. It gives you stature, quality and an inner dimension. A man without worship is a man with a flat mind. A nation which has lost the art of worship is a pedestrian, small-minded people. Worship makes for bigness of character. Worship is what Britain needs today.

Many of you must know the experience of entering an aircraft at the airport on a grey, blustery day with a fine rain blowing in your face. And in half an hour you are up above the clouds in golden sunshine, looking down on a beautiful cushion of what looks like cotton wool or thistledown.

Worship is supposed to transport us to a like vantage point. And when it does, how small today's worry seems, how stupid to fret too much over what some man said in his fit of anger. Everything looks so different under the aspect of eternity. And that is what worship is designed to do for us: cause us to see today's small worries in the light of God's great eternity.

4. *The way to start*

How do we start? Christ has told us. 'I am the way, the truth and the life.' The way to the eternal perspective is by faith in Jesus Christ. Faith takes our feet off the ground. Then we face people and problems in a new way. Yes, God the Father, God the Son, God the Holy Spirit, God in all his aspects is involved in one man finding his way to worship. At that point there is no dead-end, no final buffer stop.

AFTER TRINITY

Man's inner conflict

> Galatians 5.17 (NEB) '*That nature sets its desires against the Spirit . . . they are in conflict. . . .*'

I begin by asking what on the surface seems a silly question. What is a man? But a little reflection soon shows that it is a profound question. Especially in the twentieth century, billions of words have been written in attempting to formulate an answer. Is a man, for all his apparent superiority, basically an animal? And the answer is 'yes'. He has instincts and appetites like an animal. But looked at another way he seems more like a god, chiefly in his accomplishments, and not least in technology.

Perhaps we could describe this dichotomy in man by referring to his carnal nature and his spiritual nature. Let us look at each in turn.

1. *Carnal nature*

First, man's *carnal nature.* What this means is that man is a creature of fleshly instincts and appetites like the animals. We may call it man's lower nature, but we must not thereby judge it adversely. Man's carnal nature is a-moral, it is neither good nor bad in itself. It is raw material. And this fact of man's carnality must be accepted. One feature of it is the sex instinct. Sex does not represent the whole of our carnality, and sex is not wholly carnal, but sex is a given factor in man's nature which must be accepted without rebellion. Our Victorian grandparents found this acceptance difficult. They were largely ashamed of sex and tried to draw a veil over it. That this was a wrong attitude partly explains the violence of the twentieth-century reaction.

2. *Spiritual nature*

But man is not only carnal, he is *spiritual.* That is to say, unlike the animals, he thinks and not only has ideals but actually pursues them, sometimes at cost to himself, as for example, in altruistic action, and supremely in martyrdom. If it is stupid to ignore man's carnality and to disrespect it, it is equally stupid to underrate his spirituality.

3. *Conflict*

And now a third point. There is a *conflict* in man between his carnality and his spirituality. This internal conflict is man's burden. The fashion nowadays is to neglect it or deny it. The argument runs that whatever is natural (carnal) is able to look after itself. Control is unnecessary, and repression is wrong. Even the sex act is permissible on the public stage because it is an aspect of human experience. Whatever is natural is right. In other words, man's inner conflict need not be taken seriously.

What are we to say to this? We are to say that although neither man's carnal nature nor his spiritual nature are to be despised, the only way of successful living is for the spiritual to master the carnal. See this in the form of an analogy. Here is a horse and rider. The horse is a good thing. The rider is likewise good. Neither can do without the other if significant progress beyond man's walking pace is to be achieved, but the rider must control the horse. Heaven knows what would happen if the horse controlled the rider!

At this point it will be obvious to those acquainted with the New Testament that what I have been expounding is Paul's analysis of the human predicament. To the Christians in Galatia he wrote 'I mean this: if you are guided by the Spirit you will not fulfil the desires of your lower nature. That nature sets its desires against the Spirit, while the Spirit fights against it. They are *in conflict* with one another so that what you will to do you cannot do'. (Galatians 5.16, 17). And in the letter to the Romans, the description is even stronger. '. . . I perceive that there is in my bodily members a different law, fighting against the law that my reason approves. . . . Miserable creature that I am. . . .' (Romans 7.23, 24).

Here for a moment let me digress. I have spoken about sex as part of man's carnality or lower nature. The Church is frequently charged with making too much of sexual aberrations as if they were the chief sins. The point does need watching. Financial exploitation is also an evil bringing untold suffering in its wake. But the sex instinct is not a *minor* part of man's carnality. Freud has shown us this and writers from Sophocles to Dante, Shakespeare and Flaubert, and in his way D. H. Lawrence have testified to the uniqueness of sex in the province of human activity. They are wrong who assert that sex is a trivial matter, why make such a fuss about it? If our carnality, to be profitable, needs the control of the spiritual, this certainly applies to sex.

4. *The gospel needed*

But what sort of control? Censorship, prosecution? The application of legal restraints? St Paul was the first to despair of what the law could effect. What St Paul proclaimed was a gospel of the Spirit, God's Spirit, Christ's Spirit. This is the word of God addressed to the human psychological conflict. This Spirit needs to be spread in the community, but it begins with individuals. The man who opens his life trustingly or, to use the old technical language, 'in faith' to as much as he knows of Christ there comes the reinforcement of God's Spirit to deliver him out of his struggle, and make him a strong integrated person, neither despising his nature nor letting it master him. The Christian is in fact a disciple of Christ, learning to be a master, and before he can master anything he must master himself. The rider must be in control of the horse.

AFTER TRINITY

The work of the Spirit

Galatians 5.22 (NEB) '*But the harvest of the Spirit is love, joy, peace, patience, kindness, goodness, fidelity, gentleness, and self-control.*'

How impossible! How impossible if a Christian has to keep this list before him and wonder each day if he has managed to achieve even a modest proportion of these nine virtues. We might imagine him ticking each item like a shopping list. 'Yes, I produced some joy today, but I fell down on kindness! I didn't do too badly over peace, but I muffed it with respect to patience! But then look how difficult that wretched man in the office was when I only asked him to fetch the letters.' If this is the kind of daily self-examination required of a Christian, who would be a Christian?

The facts are, however, that this is *not* how St Paul thought of these virtues in the Christian life at all. This is clear from the key-word 'harvest'. Instead of trying to *engineer* love, joy, peace, etc., in our behaviour, we are expected to do nothing specific except to look for them to *grow*. After all, when the field has been ploughed, harrowed and rolled, the seed is planted and left. It is the winds, the rain and the warm sunshine that cause the seeds to develop. No harvest comes by tinkering with sown seed. It must be left to grow by itself.

1. *The gifts of God's grace*

This is the point. Lying in all men are the dormant gifts of all the virtues. They are all possible. They are there. The key word is *gifts*. We do not have to work for them; just as we do not have to work for our salvation, it is a gift. It comes by way of opening our lives in faith or trust to God made known in Christ. Then the eternal life is there within our very persons. So too, and following this initial and renewed response, as we expose ourselves to God's Spirit (God's wind, God's breath), in prayer, worship and all the other means of grace (charis), so the gifts of grace (the charismata), grow and increase till they produce a harvest. The harvest does not come by man's working, but by the divine Spirit's action. When we are open to God then these virtues begin to appear. They are not, therefore, so much marks of maturity as signs of our openness to God.

2. *The purpose of the gifts*

And what is the purpose of the gifts? To enhance the one who exhibits them? Not at all; but to help build up the body of Christ, which is the whole company of God's people. The gifts, the virtues, are there in every man and sometimes they blossom without his knowing (as seen in the Parable of the Sheep and the Goats, Matthew 25), but the harvest comes when the Spirit of God is allowed to be as in God's created order—mighty in operation.

AFTER TRINITY

Love

Galatians 5.22 (NEB) '. . . *the harvest of the Spirit is love.*'

Here is a church 'all at sixes and sevens'. The vicar is at loggerheads with the churchwardens. Some members of the congregation support the vicar, others support the churchwardens. The meetings of the Parochial Church Council resemble nothing so much as a slanging match. Some members resign in a huff. Others are deeply pained at the way everything seems to have turned out in the parish. And it all began through some 'locum' who came to do duty while the vicar was away. Then the bishop stepped in and wrote a strongly-worded pastoral letter to the congregation reminding them that 'the harvest of the Spirit is love'. That letter was a bit of a rebuke, but it brought everybody to their senses, they began to grasp what their true priorities were.

I have made this up, of course. I have no particular church or case in mind. What I have done is to repaint in modern colours the situation in the Church of Galatia which made St Paul write his stiff letter. It is here the phrase occurs, 'the harvest of the Spirit is love'. Then we can learn the lessons. What are they?

1. *Love is the first product of a Church*

It is an important word, this word 'product'. We hear it a great deal nowadays—productivity agreements, rising productivity, products for export. What should be the first product of a church? What should be the outcome of responding in faith to the grace of God whereby the Spirit of God is given a chance to become active in the personal life of a community? Is it a crowded church with queues to get in? Is it *four-figure* donations to undeveloped countries? Is it forms of worship that take your breath away for very loveliness? The answer is, the first product should be love between persons.

It is an answer which could be a standing rebuke to a congregation or a whole Church. Is love its outstanding characteristic?

2. *Christian love is distinctive*

As soon as I say this some one wants to reach for his hat and go home. He thought as much. Love as Christians see it is some milk-and-water affair with no real body in it. It is along the lines of the German proverb 'Jedermann's Freund ist niemands Freund'—'The friend of everybody is the friend of nobody.' But that is not so. The Bible recognizes all kinds of love, from the sort which knocks a man off his balance till he can get the girl he has no right to marry into his bed, to the sort which lays down his life for some other man. What the Christian response does is to introduce into love at all levels a different kind of love, so different that the New Testament brought into use a neglected word to describe it. The word is AGAPÉ. What it means is love concentrating wholly on giving satisfaction to the other person and not grasping it for yourself, indeed, not seeking it at all. Think what a difference that attitude would make if it was injected into a man's relationship with a girl, a mother's treatment of her son, an employee's response to his boss. AGAPÉ is revolutionary. It utterly changes interpersonal relationships at all levels. St Paul said '. . . the harvest of the Spirit is AGAPÉ.'

3. *Three directions of love*

There are three directions, that is, three patterns, along which love expresses itself when it is the response of the Christian in faith to the grace of God, and there is an order of priorities here. First, love towards God, which means in practice, service of God, self-sacrificing service. Second, love of the brethren, love among the members of a church, indeed among the members of the churches, that is, across denominational barriers. Thirdly, love towards our neighbours who may be black, white, semitic, atheistic or hippies. Which being the case it is obvious that love of a distinctive quality will be required as an impetus. This is what the Spirit provides and where love of this sort is obviously not active, doubt about the reality of the Christian response is not to be wondered at.

APPLICATION

Could we assert that there is a harvest in our church? Could we affirm that we have truly responded to the grace of God in Christ? Is it evident by the test of this verse that the Spirit of God is working visibly in our midst?—'. . . . the harvest of the Spirit is love.'

AFTER TRINITY

Joy

> Galatians 5.22 (NEB) '. . . . *the harvest of the Spirit is . . . . joy.*'

Towards the end of January the wind veered to the south-west and the barometer rose. This pushed up the temperature beyond 10°C and we rejoiced unexpectedly in a spring-like day. Anyway three children rejoiced in it two doors from mine. They rejoiced in it so loudly that I could scarcely concentrate on my work at my desk. And when I craned my neck out of my study window to see what they were doing, I saw two little girls and a boy playing follow-my-leader, their comments even more lively than their actions. What I was witnessing was an exhibition of joy.

Joy is a very elusive experience. You can't, for instance, command it. You can't shout to some one 'Oh for goodness' sake be joyful.' What I mean is, it will not make any difference in the production of happiness if you try. Nor can you work it up in yourself, nor organize it in a community, nor can you preserve joy by any manner of means; if you try to do so you only freeze it out. Here is a situation where refrigeration is no preservative. Joy comes and goes just as the sunlight on a lake comes and goes with the passage across the sun of the clouds.

1. *The future fulness of joy*

But it is wonderful to experience joy, so wonderful maybe that at such times we have said, 'Oh if only life could go on like this for ever'. That would be the fulness of joy with all the fleetingness gone for ever. The message of the Bible, however, both in the Old Testament and in the New, is that such will be the condition of life beyond the grave in God's presence. Psalm 16.12 reads, 'Thou shalt show me the path of life; in thy presence is the fulness of joy: and at thy right hand there is pleasure for ever more.' And if the future reference of this Psalm might be queried by some, we have Revelation chapter 19 verses 6 and 7. 'And I heard as it were the voice of a great multitude. . . . saying "Hallelujah: for the Lord our God, the Almighty reigneth. Let us rejoice and be exceeding glad and let us give the glory unto him." ' That in itself is a strong consolation. One day our fleeting experiences of joy will be fulfilled in a glorious permanency.

2. *Christ's joy*

Yet not even this promise exhausts the Bible's message about joy. It says that that future fulfillment may partly be realised now. It is realised in the coming of Christ. With every great act of his life on earth joy burst out. Angels appeared at his birth chanting 'Glory to God in the highest and on earth peace, goodwill among men'. And with every miracle, every parable, joy was the outcome in someone's life. His resurrection, his ascension, the coming of the Spirit produced joy. A characteristic word on his lips was 'Be of good cheer'. And the early Christians 'did take their food with gladness and singleness of heart'. (Acts 2.46). Joy then was something which Jesus imparted to his followers. And so it is that in union with him by faith the Christian today experiences in himself something of that fulfilled joy which belongs essentially to the coming of God's kingdom. In communion with Christ we partake of Christ's Spirit, the Holy Spirit, and 'the harvest of the Spirit' as St Paul said 'is joy' the joy of the life to come realised *now*.

3. *Joy in tribulation*

And one more remarkable fact about Christian joy, is that it can even be the outcome of difficulties and hardships. It was possible for St Paul to speak of joying in his tribulations. This sounds almost impossible till we remember that a mother would cheerfully suffer on behalf of her child, counting it a joy to do so, so great is her love. Similarly, love of Christ can produce joy in suffering on his behalf. This is what the martyrs knew. It is what thousands of less exalted Christians than they have known. There is such a thing as joy in tribulation for Christ's sake. This is the harvest of the Spirit.

In his book called *One Day in the Life of Ivan Denisovitch* (first published in the Soviet Union in 1962), Alexander Solzhenitsyn lets us peer into the frightening harshness of life in a Siberian labour camp. And when we are almost sickened by the depths to which human beings can sink, both captors and captured, at the end of the book there stands this sentence, ' "Oh but you mustn't pray for that either" said Aloyosha, horrified. "Why do you want freedom? In freedom your last grain of faith will be choked with weeds. You should rejoice that you are in prison. Here you have time to think about your soul. As the Apostle Paul wrote: 'Why all these tears? Why are you trying to weaken my resolution? For my part I am ready not merely to be bound, but even to die for the name of the Lord Jesus.' " '*

* * *

Perhaps after all, joy is not so fleeting an experience as we imagine. In Christ joy need never be far below the surface. Our consciousness of Christ's nearness is the underlying secret.

* Penguin edition, 1970, page 140.

AFTER TRINITY

Peace

Galatians 5.22 (NEB) '. . . *the harvest of the Spirit is . . . peace.*'

INTRODUCTION

Twice every day about twenty of us met together in the dining room of a small hotel in Denmark overlooking the straits between that country and Sweden. We did not talk much, not only because we were seated at separate tables, but because we represented many different nationalities, and language presented a problem. From time to time, however, amusing incidents took place, sometimes over the strange food that was provided and how it should be eaten. After a few days we observed that one couple nearby seemed to see the same jokes as we saw, and somehow we felt drawn to them in this unusual setting. One day when we were all sitting in the garden a shower of rain caused us all to run for whatever shelter we could reach. So we found ourselves in a kind of summer-house alone with this other couple. There was nothing for it but to talk, glad of an enforced opportunity. But it wasn't easy. English was useless. French worse. So it had to be German. And when I asked the man if he had ever visited our country he said 'Yes, Coventry, Liverpool and Bristol, but I did not see them nor set foot there.' And when my eyebrows went up in uncomprehending surprise, he replied, 'I was dropping bombs on them in the war.' This was the couple to whom all unknowingly we had felt drawn! The incident underlined for us again the stupidity of war.

War is always stupid, stupid between nations, stupid between members of a local community or a family, stupid in an individual's own life, his reason and his emotions warring against the other, so that he is a divided man. Yet it takes more than reason to do away with war. Intelligence and reasonable actions are not the simple requirements to bring about a state of peace. And for one basic reason, people do not operate solely on a basis of reason.

1. *Peace is God's gift*

Peace, then, as the Bible understands it, is not an achievement of man's ingenuity, it is a gift which comes from God, something to be enjoyed only in so far as we are willing to *receive* it. In this sense it is like love, something we accept from God and therefore something which we exercise in return to God and towards our fellowmen. Our duty towards our neighbour follows from our duty towards God. This is the order of priorities, an important order.

First we have to grasp the fact that God speaks to us. His is a reconciling word. He speaks peace to those who are afar off and to those who are near. The Cross of Christ is the place of this utterance. It is for us to hear it and believe it and live at peace with God in consequence, for he has forgiven us our sins. The case is not so much that we make our peace with God as that he makes the conditions of peace for us and we are called to accept them.

2. *To spread peace is the Christian's duty*

Because of this reconciling word of God to us the Church possesses a reconciling word to mankind and should proclaim it. This is the essence of preaching. And not only should the Church preach peace but live peace; live it firstly among church members, that is, members of all Churches, but also as far as is possible 'live peaceably with all men'. This is why the Church must always be at the front in every effort to promote peace in the world. War may temporarily drive people to their knees but it does not permanently advance the cause of the Gospel of Christ.

CONCLUSION

Peace then is 'the harvest of the Spirit'. It is not the harvest of intelligence. The roots of peace stretch down far deeper than the human mind into the love of God who offers us his peace. The call is to accept it and to practise it. Jesus said

> 'How blest are the peacemakers;
> God shall call them his sons.'
>
> (Matthew 5.9 NEB)

AFTER TRINITY

Patience

> Galatians 5.22 (NEB) '. . . *the harvest of the Spirit is . . . patience.*'

No doubt you have overheard at some time or other a conversation which ran thus: 'Of course, he ought not to have married her. She is just plain silly; that is the kindest remark you can make about her. She says such silly things, and in company too. And she does such silly things—I mean like forgetting to order the marmalade or weekend joint. But Jimmy is marvellous, never loses his temper. He is endlessly *patient* with her. I don't know how he does it.'

There is a story like this behind one of the books of the Old Testament, only stronger. That is to say, the woman married was not 'just silly' but turned out to be bad. She drifted clean out of the marriage; went off with other men, not one or two, but dozens of them, becoming in the end no better than a tart. But her husband got her home. That was the amazing fact, but not nearly as amazing as was his *longsuffering* over her; because she did not really make good again in spite of his constant love. She was always going off on some wild escapade. Yet his attitude never wavered. Something like that lies behind the book of Hosea in the Old Testament.

You will notice that in these two stories I have changed the word for the man's attitude towards his wife. In the first story it was 'patience' and in the second story I used rather an old-fashioned word, 'longsuffering'. The reason for the change is that patience was required by the husband in both instances, but in the second case the woman did not merely irritate him by silliness, she actually hurt him by her disloyalty. So the stronger word suggests pain, longsuffering, although the basic meaning is the same—patience.

1. *God's patience*

St Paul tells us that patience or longsuffering is 'the harvest of the Spirit'. If anybody ought to know it was he. St Paul was not phlegmatic. On the contrary, he could easily 'blow his top off'. And he must have felt like doing so a hundred times over these Galatians to whom he was writing. He had preached to them the gospel of justification by faith and many had responded, forming a Church alive in the freedom of the Spirit. And then some Judaizers had turned up preaching another gospel altogether, something about the necessity for all men to become Jews before they could be Christians. That meant circumcision, Jewish food-taboos, regulations about clothes and concerning the Sabbath, in fact a great burden of observances *prior* to faith in Christ. And some of the Galatians had been fool enough to believe it. And away went all their liberty, joy and attractiveness. Paul felt mad with them and the letter he wrote to them did not altogether conceal his anger. But he remembered something all Christians ought to remember. God is longsuffering. God is patient with us. He does not treat us strictly on the basis of justice but lets his mercy overrun it, giving us the opportunity to change our minds over our rebelliousness towards him. Because God is patient with our failings, we must be patient with our fellow-Christians, yes and with all men. That is to say, we must not be quick to condemn.

2. *The Church's patience*

What this means in practice is that we must not be in a hurry to turn people out of the Christian fellowship because they are not all they should be. Silly church members or bad church members should be tolerated as long as possible even though they are 'thorns in our sides'. Excommunication should be as rare among the people of God as it is with God himself. And that is one of the reasons why we have to be very careful how we work church rules and rubrics. They can be used as levers to get rid of awkward members. They can be operated to the detriment of patience.

CONCLUSION

A Church should always be patient with children (who may be adults), and longsuffering with the wayward. There are limits of course, but they are a very long way off. We have to put up with suffering for a long time before we reach the limits. That is why the word *long*suffering is appropriate. Such patience is not easily obtained but it is one of the marks of the Spirit's action in a community, it is part of 'the harvest of the Spirit'. So don't look for a pure Church without any blemishes in it, otherwise you will know that its patience has died. And where there is no patience, there is no operation of the Holy Spirit of God.

AFTER TRINITY

Kindness

> Galatians 5.22 (NEB) ' . . . *the harvest the Spirit is . . . kindness.*'

1. *Kind things*

When you are enjoying excellent food, as I hope sometimes you do, or for that matter a glass of wine, I wonder with what words you compliment it? Do you say 'This food is "super" or "smashing", or maybe that is what you used to say, for fashions change in slang almost as quickly as with women's clothes. You might even invent a word like 'scrumptious'. The word the Greeks used on these occasions was 'kind'. They said the wine was 'kind'. We have a case of this usage in the New Testament (Luke 5.39), where speaking of the wine, it is said the old is 'chrestos', that is, kind or good.

Another interesting use of this word 'kind' in the New Testament is in the words of Jesus where he says (Matthew 11.30), 'for my yoke is chrestos', that is, kind, translated 'easy' (NEB 'good to bear'). In other words, Christ's yoke does not chafe or irritate, it is comfortable or efficient. We can imagine a carpenter running his fingers over a yoke recently made in his shop, and perhaps displaying it to a potential customer. 'Look, this yoke is chrestos, kind.' Perhaps Jesus the carpenter of Nazareth actually said that to some of his customers before he became a preacher.

The only other use in the New Testament of the adjective 'kind' as applied to things beside wine and a yoke is to manners. St Paul wrote to the Corinthians, a turbulent lot, 'Be not deceived: evil company doth corrupt good (the word is chrestos, i.e., kind) manners' (1 Corinthians 15.33).

2. *Kind people*

Perhaps this rarity of usage of the word 'kind' as regards things does not surprise us. We should not think of so labelling an object. The word refers to persons. But strange to say, the Bible is also very sparing in its application of this word to persons. Only once in the Old Testament is it used in the sense of a good deed (2 Samuel 2.6). And in the New Testament there is no example of it outside Christian circles except in Acts 28.2 where another word (philanthropy), is translated 'kindness'. 'The rough islanders treated us with uncommon kindness: because it was cold and had started to rain, they lit a bonfire and made us all welcome.'

3. *The kindness of God*

Over against this sparing use of the word 'kindness' as applied to things and people, the word translated 'lovingkindness' as applied to God occurs thirty-eight times in the Old Testament.

What does this mean? It means that kindness is more an

attribute of God than it is of men. Not that people apart from God never exhibit kindness. To assert this would be a travesty of the truth. Kindness, like wild flowers, often appears in the most unlikely places, in apparently barren soil and inaccessible places. Astonishing acts of kindness were performed among the troops in the trenches of France in the 1914–1918 war, sometimes by enemy soldiers. The same is true of all wars, indeed of all manner of life-situations. And this need not surprise us, because man is made in the image of God. It is most likely that the kindness of God will be reflected even on unlikely occasions.

Kindness, however, only becomes *characteristic* of a people where that people lives out its life with constant reference to God. This is because these people of God have received in their own lives the lovingkindness of God, forgiving their sins and granting them life eternal; therefore they show forth the same lovingkindness to other people. They reflect what they already know.

4. *The origin of kindness*

Kindness then is a product of God's Spirit operating among a community and in the individual life. Kindness is part of the 'harvest of the Spirit' and if a church does not exhibit such a kindness it is to be wondered if the Divine Spirit is really operative there.

And what is kindness? It is like that wine you tasted which gave you such evident pleasure, or that wonderfully finished yoke that sat so easily on the back of the ox when it came out of Jesus' workshop, or those manners which so outshone the vulgarities of the Corinthians. Kindness is always attractive, always pleasant, the very opposite of sharp or severe. A church must be kind or it is no proper church of the Lord Jesus Christ.

Goodness

Galatians 5.22 (NEB) '*... the harvest of the Spirit is ... goodness.*'

During the autumn there was a bumper crop of apples and the Bramleys did especially well, producing large and rosy fruit far beyond the average. So I stocked up the shelves in the garden shed before the onset of winter, hoping thus to provide a supply throughout the months until the spring. But an eye has to be kept on apples, especially if the temperature in the shed drops much below 45° F. Each week the layers of fruit must be checked, especially any apples that may have been bruised. Only *good fruit* will last, only sound apples will survive the winter, and they only will continue to look appetizing.

In the Bible the word 'goodness' is applied to things like fruit and fruit trees, and it is applied to people. It is even applied to God. The word can be used to denote an aesthetic judgement; something is good to behold or it is good to taste. Or on the other hand it may be used of a moral judgement; a man's character is good, his actions are good. And the meaning involves soundness and wholesomeness, freedom from blemishes. It is with such ideas in mind that some one may be described as a good man.

1. *The goodness of God*

The Bible, however, does not expatiate on man's natural goodness, nor does it assert that man is wholly bad. Any doctrine of original sin interpreted in such terms certainly does not derive from the Bible. Man may be, certainly is, 'corrupt' in all his parts, that is to say, no part is free from taint, not even his brain. No part of his personality is perfect, but that is another matter. What the Bible is at pains to teach is that goodness belongs essentially to God. It is reflected in man in various degrees of imperfection but its origin is God himself.

And so goodness is looked for, expected and even called for among those people who are actively in touch with God by faith. Goodness should be a marked characteristic of the church where the Spirit of God dwells. And this can be when we open ourselves, as if we were windows, to that divine atmosphere by responding to Christ, a response made by faith, trust and self-commitment.

2. *Wholesomeness*

Then we are on the road to becoming good men. There is something wholesome about a good man. We may speak about a good cricketer or a good lawyer or a good motor-mechanic; and all those men are worth their weight in gold, especially today, but each one of them may be anything but good in another department of his life. He may have broken up his own marriage. He may have an unfortunate weakness for the 'bottle', he may have and exhibit a fiendish temper when you least expect it. A good man, however, is good throughout. He is wholesome. Touch him where you will, you will always discover soundness. It is what Jesus had in mind when he said 'By their fruits ye shall know them' (Matthew 7.16), and 'The good man out of the good treasure of his heart bringeth forth that which is good.' (Luke 6.45) Tree and fruit together make for a complete goodness. It is this wholesomeness St Paul refers to when he says 'the harvest of the Spirit is . . . goodness.'

The last three virtues in St Paul's striking phrase go together; 'the harvest of the Spirit is . . . patience, kindness, goodness. . . .' Is there any connection between them? Maybe patience or longsuffering is negative, as a patient man is one who does *not* let his anger boil over. Kindness is passive in the sense that it describes the background character to the one who is called kind. Goodness, however, is active, it reaches out to help those in need. It is difficult to visualize any man possessing any one of these virtues without the other. And that is the point about the man, about a community, in which the Spirit of God operates, there is a remarkable wholeness everywhere observable.

AFTER TRINITY

Fidelity

Galatians 5.22 (NEB) '*... the harvest of the Spirit is ... fidelity.*'

Many years ago (but I can remember it as if it were only yesterday), a man in my congregation came to see me. He was in deep trouble. He had 'borrowed' £80 of the firm's money and if he did not return it by the next morning he would be found out and lose his job. This would have been serious. He was married and was the son of a clergyman, but he had drifted from home and joined the Communist Party, becoming for some years a full time agent in a certain country overseas. But somehow or other he had seen the folly of his ways and returned to England to start again. He joined a Church (mine), and obtained work with an insurance firm. His father had died and then his mother was taken ill. Considering all the trouble he had caused his parents he felt that there was nothing too great he could do to help her in what proved to be her last illness. So to pay for the nursing she needed he 'borrowed' the £80 from the till, expecting to pay back the money. The day, however, dawned, as it so often does in these cases, when he knew that he would be found out. In his distress he came to me. Could I lend him £80 just to get him out of trouble! It would break his mother's heart if she knew! And if he lost his job with his record he would not easily get another. What was I to do? £80 is a large sum of money for a clergyman. And I had been let down so often over minor loans. But I wrote the cheque. I gave him £80. And he promised he would repay me at the rate of £1·50 a week. I never saw him in church again. But sure enough on Friday of the following week £1·50 arrived through the post. And the following Friday £1·50, and the Friday after that: every Friday till the whole £80 was repaid. It took a year. And when the last repayment arrived, he wrote to say he was a member of another church. Never before had I run so great a risk, never before put so much trust in a man with so little to go upon. But my trust was rewarded with outstanding fidelity; he never let me down.

1. *Fidelity not faith*

This is our subject for today—fidelity or trustworthiness. In the Authorized Version the word 'faith' is used and 'faith' is an exact translation of the word St Paul actually used in his letter. But the meaning in the letter to the Galatians is not active belief in Christ, that majestic theme of the New Testament and especially of St Paul, but the passive aspect which describes the character of the person who has that faith, in other words, 'faithfulness (RV), or 'fidelity' (NEB). A clear example can be seen in Titus 2.10 where servants are counselled to be 'strictly honest and trustworthy'.

2. *Modern infidelity*

Nowadays we see the evidence of a great deal of infidelity—in marriage, at work, in dealings with public bodies such as railway companies and insurance firms. A great deal of dishonesty prevails at all levels. And employees count it their right to help themselves to their employer's goods. Work contracts get broken and far too many people do not carry out an honest day's work. Untrustworthiness is becoming a common feature of our times.

No Christian should relax his hold on fidelity. It is at this point that there should be a marked difference between those who profess the Christian faith and those who do not. So much so that the time will not be far distant when employers will look for workers who are church-men whenever they have a task that calls for particular trustworthiness.

3. *Fidelity derives from faith*

Let us not fool ourselves. Fidelity will not grow up in a community without faith. The word 'fidelity' derives from faith. So does the virtue itself. It is the man who believes in Christ who is most likely to be faithful in everything he does. And remember faith links us to God's Spirit and it is God's Spirit working in us that produces 'the harvest of fidelity'.

AFTER TRINITY

Gentleness

Galatians 5.22 (NEB) '*... the harvest of the Spirit is ... gentleness.*'

1. *God's voice*

Of course I might have known but I have to confess I never thought of it till I attended a church famous for its music. That was years ago. Till then I had conceived of God's voice in so far as I had seriously thought about it at all as strong, awe-inspiring and commanding. And had I not something to substantiate this view? Psalm 29 reads:

'It is the Lord that commandeth the waters:
it is the glorious God that maketh the thunder.
It is the Lord that ruleth the sea; the voice
of the Lord is mighty in operation: the voice
of the Lord is a glorious voice.
The voice of the Lord breaketh the cedar trees:
Yea, the Lord breaketh the cedars of Libanus. . . .
The voice of the Lord divideth the flames of fire;
the voice of the Lord shaketh the wilderness:
Yea, the Lord shaketh the wilderness of Cades.'

Then I heard this particular choir singing the Psalms. It was an unforgettable experience. Instead of drowning chords on the organ when God's voice was being repeated and a full-throated bass chorus, there was *un*accompanied pianissimo full choir. I have never forgotten it. From then on I have remembered how God's voice is a still, small voice when it comes to dealing with people. In nature it may be in the wind, the fire and the earthquake. It may tear in pieces the rocks upon the mountains; but when a *man* is spent, broken-hearted and down, the voice of God which remakes him is unbelievably gentle. This is how the Spirit speaks.

> 'And his that gentle voice we hear,
> Soft as the breath of even,
> That checks each fault, that calms each fear,
> And speaks of heaven.'
>
> (Harriet Auber)

2. *Christ's voice*

And the Lord's servant as depicted in the famous Servant Songs was likewise gentle.

> 'He shall not cry nor lift up, nor cause
> his voice to be heard in the street.
> A bruised reed shall he not break
> And the dimly burning wick
> he shall not extinguish.'
>
> (Isaiah 42.2, 3)

And when some men of Galilee saw Jesus of Nazareth they recognized his identity through this 'Servant Song'. Jesus was strong but he was gentle too. He was the strong man who overthrew the firmly entrenched forces of evil and spoiled their goods, but he did not curse the woman taken in adultery, he did not reject the children whom his disciples would have turned away, he took them in his arms. There are few sights more moving than to see a strong, young man with a tender baby in his arms. That is a picture of the gentleness of the Lord of glory. He deals with us with tenderness.

Nor is this sloppy sentiment. The skilled artist wields his

brush with gentleness. A month ago I stood in the Spanish Room of the National Gallery watching a copy-artist at work on a Velasquez. It was amazing to see the lightness of his touch as he finished off his brilliant canvas, such gentle strokes with the lightest of hands. It was hard to see what difference his final touches were making. But they were achieving what he wished. These were the master-strokes of a skilled workman. And this is how Christ worked and how his Spirit still is working, working with the gentleness of his godly expertise.

3. *The gentleness of the Christian*

We have talked of God, we have talked of Christ, we have talked of God's Spirit and have heard of gentleness. What of the Christian? What of Christ's followers? What of the Church? What of you and what of me? Is there this gentleness? Gentleness in this current age of violence? St Paul said '. . . the harvest of the Spirit is . . . gentleness'. We need to remember this. Gentleness does not come by forcing it. Gentleness does not come by intelligence alone. Gentleness comes by catching Christ's Spirit, the Christ who did not hit back but suffered rather in his body. We have to believe in his way to achieve his way, the way of the master-artist with the souls of men. Every Christ-man must be gentle, gentle as his Lord is gentle, gentle in his strength.

AFTER TRINITY

Self-control

Galatians 5.22 (NEB) '. . . *the harvest of the Spirit is . . . self-control.*'

INTRODUCTION

I would like you to imagine for a moment an oriental scene of luxury and ease. Outside the pitiless sun is burning down on the stone-flagged streets and the tops of the houses.

Every window is shuttered to keep out the heat. But within this room there is coolness. Brightly coloured carpets cover the floor and silken cushions the couches. Outside a fountain is playing in the courtyard. The whole setting is fit for a king. Indeed, a kind of king lives there, Felix the Roman Governor with his Jewish wife Drusilla. But though the place houses luxury and an agreeable refuge from the heat, it also spells boredom to this couple. They feel the need for diversion. And they find it by summoning their servant to have Paul the prisoner, brought in. He would entertain them with his talk. And sure enough, he did. There were few more engaging talkers than Paul the Apostle. And when he talked of faith in Christ Jesus, even that was captivating. Felix the Governor could not fail to listen. But when Paul turned the talk to 'morals, *self-control* and the coming judgement', Felix became alarmed and exclaimed 'That will do for the present. When I find it convenient I will send for you again!' All this can be read in the Acts of the Apostles, chapter 24.

1. *Faith and self-control*

Felix made excuses when Paul talked of self-control. It was all right to talk about faith, all right to talk about Jesus of Nazareth, but when faith in Jesus Christ issues in morals and self-control, Felix turned aside. But faith in Jesus Christ has no substance *unless* it produces self-control. It is mere sentiment or an idea or even a day-dream; real faith must produce a difference in the behaviour of him who professes it, and this means self-control.

2. *The need for self-control*

Man is essentially a mixture. There is a lower part of his nature and a higher part, and if he is to achieve any stature as a man, the lower part has to be mastered by the higher so that there is a kind of harmony. This is what Plato emphasized in the fourth book of the *Republic* centuries before Christ. Perhaps Felix had even heard of the four virtues the Greeks stressed; Wisdom, Courage, Temperance and Justice. Perhaps he knew in his conscience that Paul was right when he stressed self-control, the other word for which is temperance. And what Paul was offering was a new way to achieve that ideal, the way of faith in Jesus Christ.

3. *The Spirit brings self-control*

And for this reason, that faith in Jesus Christ brings the Spirit of Christ into the life of the one who exercises it. And that Spirit, the Holy Spirit, strengthens the good part in the man's mixed nature, achieving harmony, self-control, temperance. This is the harvest of the Spirit.

APPLICATION

Self-control over what? Every kind of intemperance, every kind of appetite—over eating, over drinking, over anger, over laziness, over sex, over pleasure. Every kind of excess is a fall away from the Christian ideal of living. Pre-eminently a Christian must be a balanced man, a balanced woman, still a man, still a woman, more of a man, more of a woman, because intemperance degrades. What a shining light this self-control was in the world where Paul called out his first Christians. That old pagan world was full of orgies of excess. What a shining light the balanced Christian is in our world today. Truly the harvest of the Spirit is self-control. And Christ offers it to every one.

ALL SAINTS' DAY

God's family

For many years now I have made a habit of calling on as many lonely people as I can fit in on Christmas Eve. In practice this turns out to be a string of elderly ladies, for the very simple reason that they tend to live longer than men. I do this for obvious reasons. Christmas is the family season. We are reminded of this by various recurring phrases. 'I went to my family last Christmas; my daughter will be coming to me this year.' 'Unfortunately my family was laid up with the 'flu at Christmas and I had nowhere to go.' So when bereavement or frailty means 'no family for Christmas' many elderly folk find this particularly hard to bear. So I pay my call on Christmas Eve. It helps, I think, a little.

1. *Belonging is necessary*

We all need a family. At least we all possess a need to belong. It is a frightening experience to hear the screech of car brakes in the street, to rush out and see an old man knocked over. You pick him up, lift him on to the pavement, wonder who he can be, search his pockets for identification marks, then the police arrive; there is nothing to tell who he is, he doesn't seem to belong to anybody. . . !

Everybody needs to belong. And if we have no family surviving, there needs to be a club or a society or a community-centre where we count for something. Every one has been born into a relationship with someone else, and we can never get this out of our systems. And you will notice that the first information we are given about God becoming incarnate in human life in St Matthew's Gospel, the first book of the New Testament, is information about *his family tree*.

2. *The Church as a family*

This is the thought to which I want now to lead you. God entered *our* family in the person of Jesus. We can enter into God's family through the same gateway. And what is his family? At All Saints' tide it is 'a great multitude, which no man could number, of all nations, and kindreds, and people and tongues, stood before the throne, and before the Lamb, clothed with white robes, and palms in their hands. . . .' God's family is, in fact, the Church in heaven, and not only that, but the Church on earth. God's family encompasses that vast family of people who have lived and died, and died and live, and still live, not yet having died, all, a vast company, who have become God's children by faith in Jesus Christ. That is the family we think of at All Saints' tide, the family we enter by adoption, whoever we may be.

I have stressed the importance, the necessity, of belonging. Every man, to be wholesome, must belong somewhere. And I want to stress the importance of belonging to God's family. Do not misunderstand me. This is not another way of asserting that it is good psychologically for a man to belong to the club called the Church, if he knows no other organization which attracts him. I am thinking of the time when the very foundations of our life disintegrate and we know that as far as this world is concerned, we are nearing the end. At that time it is reassuring to know that we belong to God's family, the family which death does not break up, the family which stretches across *both* sides of the frontier-post we call the grave. We belong to that family by faith, its members are the people of Christian faith, but that faith needs to be marked outwardly by the sign which is baptism, the public expression of belonging.

3. *Mark your membership of God's family*

Let us therefore end on a practical note. Make sure you belong to God's family, that is, make your membership sure. Make it sure by faith. Make it sure by baptism. God is waiting to adopt you. No-one is too old to believe, no one too old to be baptized. And keep your membership fresh in that family by means of the Holy Communion. The sacraments are means of grace. We need these outward signs and symbols, we need assurances that we belong.